D0129119

COUNTER CULTURE
TEXAS

COUNTER CULTURE
TEXAS

Susie Kelly Flatau

and

Mark Dean, Photographer

Republic of Texas Press

Library of Congress Cataloging-in-Publication Data

Flatau, Susie Kelly.
   Counter culture Texas / Susie Kelly Flatau; Mark Dean, photographer.
     p. cm.
   ISBN 1-55622-737-X (pb.)
   1. Restaurants--Texas Guidebooks. 2. Restaurants--Texas Pictorial works.
   I. Dean, Mark.   II. Title.
   TX907.3.T4F553   1999
   647.95764—dc21   99-26667
                                                CIP

Republic of Texas Press is an imprint of Wordware Publishing, Inc.
No part of this book may be reproduced in any form or by
any means without permission in writing from
Wordware Publishing, Inc.

Printed in the United States of America

ISBN 1-55622-737-X
10 9 8 7 6 5 4 3 2 1
9909

All inquiries for volume purchases of this book should be addressed to Wordware Publishing, Inc., at 2320 Los Rios
Boulevard, Plano, Texas 75074. Telephone inquiries may be made by calling:

(972) 423-0090

Acknowledgments

Special thanks are given to—
Karen Fitzjerrell and Nancy Snyder for their time and editorial expertise,
Jack and Jenni for their loving support and patience,
friends for their encouragement,
and most importantly
the truly wonderful Texans who shared their
hearts, stories, and counters.

Susie Kelly Flatau

To Rita and Bill, for my upbringing and all
of the opportunities to live, learn, and love.

Mark "Dink" Dean

Key to Counter Culture Texas Locations

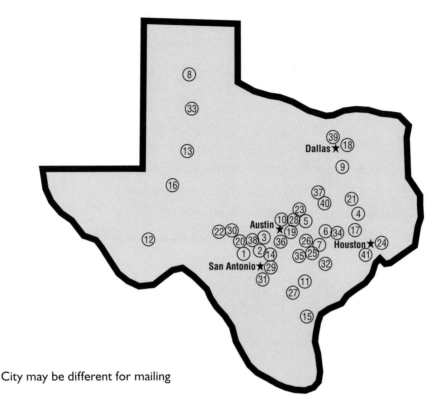

City may be different for mailing

1 Arkey Blue's Silver Dollar
Bandera

2 Bergheim
General Store
Bergheim

3 Blanco Bowling
Club Cafe
Blanco

4 Cafe Texan
Huntsville

5 Cele General Store
Manor

6 Citizens Pharmacy
Brenham

7 Charlie's Bar-B-Q
Smithville

8 Cope's Coney Island
Canyon

9 Dee's Place
Corsicana

10 Dirty Martin's Place
Austin

11 Doll House Cafe
Cuero

12 Girvin Social Club
Girvin

13 Green Hut Cafe
Lamesa

14 Gruene Hall
Gruene

15 Hamlin Pharmacy
Corpus Christi

16 Henderson Collins
Soda Fountain and
Malt Shop
Odessa

17 Henry's Hideout
Fetzer

18 Highland Park
Pharmacy
Dallas

19 Hut's Hamburgers
Austin

20 Ingenhuett Store
Comfort

21 Ken Martin's
Walker Pharmacy
Madisonville

22 Kitty's Place
Ingram

23 Knebel's Tavern
Pflugerville

24 La Carafe
Houston

25 Leon's Country Store
Rockne

26 Lock Drugs
Bastrop

27 Midway Bar
Yorktown

28 Old Times Bar & Grill
Rice's Crossing

29 Olmos Pharmacy
San Antonio

30 Pampell's Antiques
& Soda Fountain
Kerrville

31 Patt's Drug Store
San Antonio

32 Pavlas Tavern
Moulton

33 Quick Lunch
Plainview

34 Randermann's
Brenham

35 Red Rock
General Store
Red Rock

36 Scholz Garten
Austin

37 Sefcik Hall
Seaton

38 Sisterdale
General Store
Sisterdale

39 Sonny Bryan's
Smokehouse
Dallas

40 Tex Miller's
Cameron

41 Yale Street Grill & Gifts
Houston

CONTENTS

Contents

FOREWORD

When we hit the winding back roads of Texas to begin work on *Counter Culture Texas*, a desire to experience real places—places where people meet and spend quality time together, places where conversations occur at an unhurried pace—drove us. We wanted to discover locales that felt more like a living room than a business office, where a sense of comfort hugged you the moment you walked through the door. And the one binding thread throughout our mission was that we were searching for places with old counters that still serve as focal points in the lives of Texans and which personify the term small business in an age of fast food and corporate chains.

Little did we know as we began our journey that the phrase "If you don't look, you won't see!" would become the underlying theme of our book. We casually traveled the numerous Texas back roads, often without any direction other than the handy road map, a suggestion by someone we had met, or a personal whim, and as we did so we found and connected with some of the most wonderful people and places that Texas has to offer. Throughout our travels we were welcomed into their worlds to listen to their stories, to record their firsthand knowledge of the business' history, to eat their food or drink their drinks, and ultimately to enjoy their counters over which so much neighborliness has occurred.

Ironically, in spite of the number of establishments with counters that still exist, we realized they are slowly disappearing as the small town family-run business must compete with the high-volume mass-market arena.

Therefore, we vowed that before we turn the page to the next millenium we would capture these Texas treasures in a volume of work. We feel we have accomplished this through casual, journal-style sketches that integrate elements of the places, people, and on-the-spot oral history interviews combined with black-and-white photographs.

It is with a great sense of loss, however, that we have learned some of these Texas treasures are now a thing of the past. On your next drive down the freeway, listen to your inner voice as it urges you to forego the beaten path and drive through the townships instead of taking the bypass. We hope you are able to experience firsthand the places included in *Counter Culture Texas* and that you have the good fortune to sit and visit with these interesting folks. Or perhaps, you will discover some treasures of your own. Believe us, it is worth it.

Susie Kelly Flatau
Mark Dean

La Carafe

LA CARAFE

*While most people were celebrating our country's independence
with fireworks, barbecues, and family gatherings, we were following
a lead about a local historical bar located in downtown Houston.
Pulling up curbside at 813 Congress we spotted only two other
parked cars. I thought to myself, "Not a bad turnout at La Carafe,
considering this is the 4th of July."*

Decorative wrought iron adorned the building's single front window only to be mirrored by a massive iron gate which guarded the entrance to the side alleyway. The structure's red bricks, powdered with age, were meticulously garnished with forest green trim. Above the door hung an ornately carved sign. This impressive door, its mail slot, and its iron locks and bolts added further character to the bar's old-world image.

As I walked into the narrow room, the day's humidity evaporated into a cellar-like coolness. When the door closed, I found myself bathed in natural light that filtered in from the front window and commingled with the amber radiance of the interior lights and lamps.

A large moose head mounted high on the front wall kept an eye on the room. Below this regal creature stood a wooden table carved with names and dates. Upon the brick-and-plaster side wall hung clusters of old photos which framed the oil portrait of an elegantly posed woman. Five small tables offered intimate, snug settings.

Sitting atop a brick base, a long counter that ran the length of the room's other side also chronicled visits by patrons whose names had been deeply etched into the counter's thick pine. Along that same counter beer mugs held candles that daintily flickered as ceiling fans turned at a turtle's pace. Fourteen barstools provided seating.

All forms of foreign paper money peppered the aged wood of the back bar, a custom that began in the early 1980s when two men placed a bet about the motion of the solar system. One man took a ten dollar bill, tore it in two, and pinned one half on the back bar; he then saved the other half to be taped later to its mate when the bet was resolved. Although the bet was never settled, the act of taping foreign currency onto the bar continues to be put in practice either by visitors to the United States or by Americans traveling abroad.

At either end of the back bar were two satyr sculptures that stood like silent stone sentinels of La Carafe's fine wine. To the inside of each sculpted guardian reigned candles festooned with fold upon fold of frozen wax that represented twenty-five years of candlelight encounters. Positioned between this pair of waxen towers was a 1907 brass cash register.

A staircase at the room's far end piqued my curiosity, and I soon explored an upstairs bar with its own unique personality. Light splashed in through three large stained glass windows and bounced colors

off the room's dark wood. To the left stood a long black-and-green marble counter which fronted an elegant back bar. In the middle of that back bar, an antique carrousel horse pranced like a snapshot in time.

Mounted deer heads and antlers hung on the walls in the midst of old black-and-white photos. Four antiquated coat-of-arm shields embellished the large oil portrait of a man who exuded the same panache as the woman presiding in the portrait downstairs. A customer had a choice of sitting at either the bar or one of the tables.

With my curiosity satisfied I then went back downstairs to speak with the bartender about La Carafe's history. He explained that around 1847 this building had housed a trading post and general store. After a fire destroyed the structure, an Irish immigrant, John Kennedy, built the first of his steam bakeries on this site in 1860.

It wasn't until the late 1950s or early 1960s, that Jim Harrison bought the business and La Carafe was born. In the mid-1960s Bill Berry, a retired air force officer, took over and brought in the majority of the English antiques one finds in the place today. Then, in 1985, Warren Trousdale secured the business. After his death a year and a half later, La Carafe was bought by Carolyn Wenglar, who remains the current owner.

After enjoying La Carafe's old-world charm, I rose to leave. With effort I pulled open the massive oak door and reluctantly stepped back into the Houston heat. Before driving away, I turned one last time to memorize the facade of this exquisite wine bar with its European flair.

La Carafe
813 Congress
Houston, TX 77002
(713) 229-9399

La Carafe

La Carafe

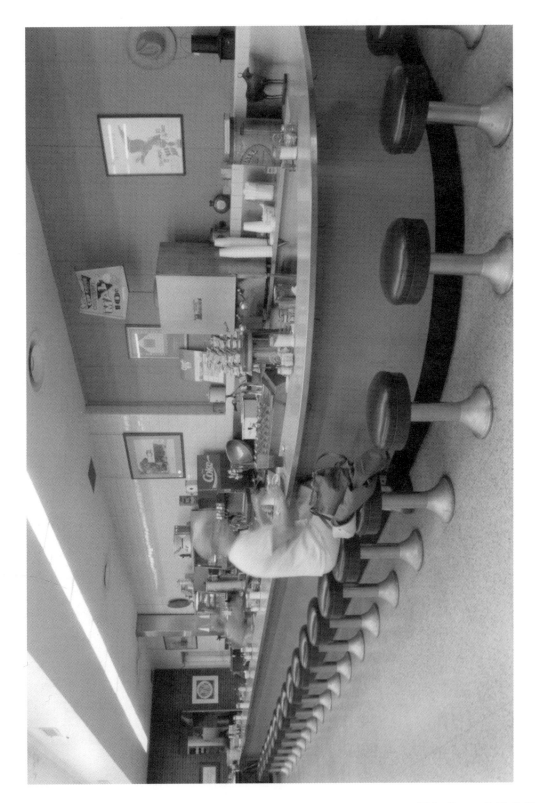

Yale Street Grill & Gifts

YALE STREET GRILL & GIFTS

On another jaunt through Houston, we made a decision to check out a rumored "seventy-year-old favorite Houston hangout" and headed for Yale Street Grill & Gifts. The first clue that those tales rang true were the fifteen cars parked in front of and alongside the grill that sat at the corner of Yale Street and 21st. A quick study of the building created a feeling of anticipation.

After pulling into the only available parking spot on the store's side, I hopped out of the car. Simultaneously I spied a fast food restaurant that sat next door, and I made a note about the cars lined up five deep in its drive-through lane which held drivers who looked like snapshots of disgruntlement and impatience.

I hoped that the Yale Street diners would not mirror the same type of angst. Upon entering the store, I immediately regarded the expansiveness of the place. The room was filled with shelves offering a wide range of gift items. The back left corner housed a postal section, and the right side was filled with customers who sat at the tables and soda fountain. No one appeared disgruntled or impatient. I breathed a sigh of relief and then examined the long counter with a blonde Formica top that started near the front door, curved slightly into the room, then ran for forty or fifty feet parallel to the side wall.

Observing that customers occupied twelve of the twenty-one barstools, I found it curious that the waitresses and cooks looked short, really short. But upon close inspection, I discovered that the floor behind the counter had been lowered, thus putting barstool customers and wait staff at eye level. I liked the way this arrangement made for easy, personable connections.

Behind the counter, stainless steel coolers, refrigerators, and sinks gleamed in cool contrast to the wall's warm yellow tile. Upon the back counter was memorabilia depicting times from yesteryear. There was a sign advertising a chocolate malt for 10¢, old photos, a five-bladed blender, and an hour-glass-shaped porcelain piece. I soon learned that this last curio, with the initials RX on the top half and the word Yale on the bottom half, was the light placed on the roof of the delivery car during the 1950s.

When I asked with whom I might speak about the store's history, our waitress pointed to the current manager, Debbie Drouin, sitting at the fountain's far end. Introductions were made, and I found Debbie happy to talk about the place. She called over her stepfather, Joc Dupuis, to join in.

Joe, who had been the former manager and pharmacist, began to recall specific historical details about the pharmacy and soda fountain. His parents, Abel and Mildred Dupuis, founded the business in 1923. At that time the pharmacy was located across the street, then in 1928 they moved down the block to another building. That store was remodeled in 1940 and later moved to its present site in 1951.

Yale Street Grill & Gifts

Debbie chimed in at that point and recalled the 1950s when they would often have one hundred to one hundred and fifty kids standing outside the old Yale Pharmacy early in the morning before school. (The business name has since been changed to Yale Street Grill and Gifts.) Joe would monitor the young crowd, allowing twenty or so kids in at first, then as two youngsters would leave he'd let in two more. She smiled and said that many of those same teenagers are now parents who bring their own children in to experience the fountain.

She mentioned one group of men in their fifties and sixties, known as the "Old Reagan High School Boys," who still come in every Wednesday. Then she added that new residents to the surrounding areas are also making Yale Grill a regular stopping-off place.

Joe went on to explain that when he started working at the pharmacy in the 1950s he handled a variety of jobs from soda jerk to delivery boy to stocker to pharmacist. With the death of his father in 1978 he added "owner" to his long resumé at the Yale establishment. He proudly pointed out that his mother, who is still involved in the family business, was one of the first Texas women pharmacists.

With that he excused himself, but before returning to work he told me to be sure to check out the photos of the old drugstores. I did so, trying to imagine each in its prime. Then I exited through the side door just in time to see a local policeman in his sky blue squad car drive up and get out. He gave a friendly wave then headed for the front door of his neighborhood hangout.

Yale Street Grill & Gifts
2100 Yale Street
Houston, TX 77008
(713) 861-3113

Henry's Hideout

HENRY'S HIDEOUT

We left Houston's hectic pace and opted for back roads that would take us away from the heart of the big city. With much anticipation we headed for Fetzer, Texas. Buildings were sparse along the two lanes of FM 1774, creating a sense of traveling into some sort of unspoiled area. We had been letting providence guide us when up ahead loomed the signpost: Henry's Hideout. Pulling onto the gravel lot, I beheld two trucks. I checked my watch. 10:45 A.M.

As I stepped out of the car, a cat sauntered toward the building's front porch where a resting German shepherd lazily lifted its head. He twitched one of his dog ears my way then obviously decided I was OK and went back to sleep. Lofty pine trees towered over the large wooden building. Their fallen pine cones crunched underfoot as I approached the porch where a man talked on a pay phone.

Inside Henry's Hideout my footfalls echoed up from the wood floors in syncopation to rock-and-roll music playing on a jukebox. Looking up, I realized I was walking beneath a ceiling that served as a canvas for literally thousands of antlers. I walked beneath those horned stalactites over to the long, L-shaped bar and took a seat at one of the nineteen mismatched barstools. Coolers lined the walls behind the counter, and knickknacks filled the shelves. Neon signs cast a prismatic glow throughout the room.

Pool tables and dining tables stood about the room, accented by walls that displayed snapshots and articles featuring the Hideout and its patrons. Everywhere I looked those same walls came alive with mounted animal bodies, heads, and skins. And there were horns everywhere. All types of horns. All shapes of horns. All sizes of horns. I laughed to myself as I recalled the bumper sticker I had seen on a post by the bar that touted Henry's Hideout as the "Horniest Place in Texas." Made sense to me now.

Swinging doors at the end of this hunter's haven led into another large dance hall built in 1964 and expanded in 1985. The room's low ceiling created an intimate arena for the tables that ran down each side of the hall. They butted up against walls plastered with a patchwork of paintings and velvet wall hangings. The slick, worn patina of the wooden dance floor traced years of shuffling feet.

I returned to the front room and noted nine more people lounging about. I checked my watch. 11:15 A.M.

Grabbing my journal, I then asked the bartender about the saloon's history. Within minutes she related how Henry Phillips had built the bar on this site when he was only eighteen years old. At that time the building was one quarter of its present size; however, Mr. Phillips continued to expand the structure in direct proportion to its growing popularity.

During Henry's fifty-five-year ownership, he was absent from the business for

Henry's Hideout

only a few years while he served in World War II. In his absence his father ran the Hideout to keep the business going. She added that another member of the Phillips family who has been part of this venture is Henry's nephew, Billy.

One of the customers added that Henry, who died in 1992, was loved by everyone and is still considered to be one of the most charitable men who ever lived around these parts. He continued by describing Henry as a "jolly fellow who people thought was good as gold."

As more patrons entered, I begged for more of the bartender's time, and in the minutes she could give me, I heard about the regulars who have been coming into Henry's Hideout for over thirty years. Taking their patronage one step further, many of those regulars represent family members who span three generations and who have made Henry's their regular haunt.

She then explained that the Texas Renaissance Festival, which has been held just down the road for over a decade, has also brought an extraordinary number of new customers to this small hideout in Fetzer. A bit confused about the exact size of Fetzer, I asked for clarification. "This is just about it," hollered a guy shooting pool. He waved his arm around the room in a broad sweeping motion and concluded, "Once you leave the grounds of Henry's Hideout, you're pretty much out of Fetzer." There were nods of agreement.

With that I pointed to the ceiling near the doorway and asked if they were finished adding antlers to it. "No way," replied the bartender. "There's a whole box of antlers in the basement right now. We'll just keep putting them up anywhere we can as long as our friends keep bringing them in."

Seeing that my time at Henry's Hideout had drawn to a close, I walked out of the bar underneath the canopy of antlers. I checked my watch—11:58 A.M.

Henry's Hideout
Route 1 Box 700
Plantersville, TX 77363
(281) 356-3538

Henry's Hideout

Henry's Hideout

Cafe Texan

CAFE TEXAN

Using Houston as a home base, we left the city around 10 A.M. in order to avoid the early morning rush-hour traffic that moves with the speed of tree sap. We drove north on Interstate 45 and passed a seemingly endless stretch of stately pine trees speckled white with blooming dogwoods. Upon arrival in Huntsville, the trip around the courthouse square offered a quick, true find when we spied the Cafe Texan.

The corner cafe's architecture blended old and new; weathered bricks were bedecked with modern canvas awnings and tall French windows. Once inside I noted the clientele ranged from business people in dress suits to university coeds in jeans and T-shirts to men in coveralls and cowboy hats. Although most of the customers at this particular time of day were men, a handful of women occupied spots at the counters and tables.

A glance about the place revealed that the cafe consisted of two adjacent rooms connected by a doorway. A pair of counters stretched down this room's left side. The one closest to the front door offered swivel-back stools covered in tan vinyl. The back counter offered a mishmash of chairs, and its location allowed for a straight shot into the kitchen to observe the cooks through the narrow serving window.

I took a seat at the first counter and ordered the cafe's famous chicken fried steak; to make the best of my time as I waited for the meal I visited the other room. I found it dark and empty. There was a serving buffet waiting to be set up for its dinner guests; there were old historical paintings and photos hanging on the walls, which enhanced the room's formal charm.

And there were tables filling every inch of the space. As I headed back to the other room I noted that a multitude of lunchtime diners had arrived.

Amid this sea of hungry patrons, a group of elderly gentlemen sat at a table near the front window; they sipped coffee and talked about the latest news. I found myself casting a sly stare at one of these gentlemen in particular as the notion that I had seen him somewhere else stirred my thoughts. However, since I couldn't pinpoint the origin of that nudging, I shrugged it off for the moment.

Around me conversations flowed easily as busy waitresses joked with one another and the customers. When the chance arose, I introduced myself to Lola Becker and asked her some questions about the establishment. I learned that thirty-one years ago Lola and a group of Illinois girls came to Texas for a visit, but when her friends returned home she stayed and has continued to work at the Cafe Texan ever since. She then talked about another coworker, Bert, who has worked at the cafe for twenty years. But to top both of those stories, she told me about Mance, who began cooking at the cafe at its grand opening in 1936 and has only recently retired.

Cafe Texan

I was trying to imagine working in one place for such a long period of time when a woman walked up and took a seat next to me. Before long Waya Hubbard, an attractive soft-spoken lady with a gentle sense of humor, eagerly shared her knowledge of the cafe's history. She traced it back to its beginning in 1936 when Fred Morris was the owner and Vernon Todd the manager. She explained that through the combined efforts of these two men during the 1930s and 1940s the place earned its long-standing reputation as being one of the best cafes in Texas.

In 1958 Vernon Todd and Joe Burns leased the business from Mr. Morris, and in 1968 Vernon assumed sole ownership and ran the cafe until 1973. After the eatery fell under different ownerships for a period of time, Waya and her husband, Paul, bought the place in April of 1995. To bring the cafe's proprietorship up to date, Waya pointed out that John Strickland now owns the business and Stacey Beck manages it.

Lola then placed my platter on the counter. Hungrily I stared at the Texas-size helpings of chicken fried steak and mashed potatoes. As I picked up my knife and fork, Lola boasted about the oil portraits that hang in the room. She praised the local artist, Julius Slaughter, who had immortalized some of the Cafe Texan's old-time regulars on canvas. And then like a museum docent, she gestured to each painting. There was Mr. Morgan, Don, Buster, Bubba, and, of course, Levi. She nodded her head in the direction of the table where the group of elderly men sat.

I followed her nod and suddenly realized where I had seen the man who earlier had captured my attention. I looked from the painting on the wall back to this man sitting at the table, and it all made sense. There, sharing tales with his cronies, sat the living, breathing gentleman who smiled down upon the customers from the painting at the other end of the room.

As I savored one of the best chicken fried steaks I had ever eaten—sorry, Mom, but it's true—I mused that any business that combines delectable food with local art of its customers is indeed not only a place of the palate but also a place of the heart.

Cafe Texan
1120 Sam Houston
Huntsville, TX 77340
(409) 295-2381

Cafe Texan

Cafe Texan

Ken Martin's Walker Pharmacy

Ken Martin's Walker Pharmacy

While we were sitting in the Cafe Texan in Huntsville, a customer told us about a pharmacy in Madisonville that had an old counter. With that carrot dangled before our noses, we headed out around 10:30 A.M. the next morning to continue the vintage voyage north on Interstate 45. It felt like a mere hop, skip, and a jump before we crossed into Madisonville's city limits. Across from the courthouse we noticed a hand-painted sign that advertised Ken Martin's Walker Pharmacy.

Once I opened the large front door, a fog of dense conversation blanketed me. The place was packed. The tables near the front windows were filled. The six barstools at the counter were occupied. The seven tables in the room's center were taken, and the two freestanding booths at the back of the dining area were claimed. Altogether, thirty-one people seemed to enjoy a very sociable lunch hour.

The four women working the counter and grill had their routines down pat. One filled drinks, another cooked, another put orders together, and the other one delivered them. Everything was made from scratch, and the patrons appeared more than willing to wait.

Looking around I noted that although the building was old, the walls were freshly painted sky blue. Old light fixtures hung down about twelve feet from the high ceiling of hammered tin, which was wreathed by carved molding. New furniture was intertwined with other pieces that revealed signs of long use.

I opened my journal and quickly sketched the large CKM brand design that stood out on the wall high above the old back bar. Underneath that drawing I then copied two bronco scenes that were also painted on the walls. One portrayed a cowboy on a cutting horse and the other a cowboy roping a steer.

Then I turned my attention to the wall above the pharmacy where a mural offered a caption that read "No, not much happens in a town like this, but the rumors sure do make up for it." I wrote the quotation in the journal and scribbled a note saying I liked a place that not only embraces a sense of humor about life but also announces it.

At that point a couple left their seats at the counter, so I grabbed one of the stools and immediately asked the waitress about the old cash register. She explained, "That's been here since the days when Van and Catherine Walker owned the pharmacy." When I asked about the counter, the young lady patted the counter's top and said, "This has been here since the Walkers' days, too, since about 1945."

A warm beauty radiated from the counter's black marble, which was filled with eddies of swirled white-and-gray strokes;

Ken Martin's Walker Pharmacy

its base consisted of the same exquisite material. Beyond the counter, I noted the back bar's beauty was enriched with beveled mirrors, stained glass side pieces, and old latch doors on the cabinets.

To learn more about the pharmacy's history, I asked the young lady for further information. Without breaking stride in her food preparation, she pointed to the man in the pharmacy and said, "You need to talk with him."

Soon Ken Martin, the current pharmacist and business owner, shared that the original business, Turner Pharmacy, opened in 1914. In 1945 Van and Catherine Walker secured the business from a Mr. Coleman and together they ran it until 1974. That was the year, Ken explained, that he bought the pharmacy and business. The building itself, however, remains in the possession of Mrs. Walker.

Several people required Ken's attention. He turned to them, and I noticed his personal connection as he greeted everyone by name. Not only did he inquire about their families, but he also listened intently to their latest life news.

I then spotted the framed photos displayed on the side wall. When I asked about them, Ken showed off the pictures of past and present employees before reaching below the counter and pulling out an overstuffed album of the reunion party he had held in honor of these employees.

A bit later Ken introduced me to Leatie Ann, who was born and reared in Madisonville and who has worked at the store for twenty-four years. She motioned for me to sit with her, and I gladly accepted. She shared many of the experiences she has had at the pharmacy, but it was her last memory that rang most poignant. She recalled how as a little girl she "had come into Walker's Pharmacy all the time and remembered it always being a happy, busy place."

This simple statement summed it up perfectly. Obviously, Walker's Pharmacy has long been a "happy, busy place" for those who enter and stay long enough to enjoy its hospitality.

Ken Martin's Walker Pharmacy
112 W. Main
Madisonville, TX 77864
(409) 348-2671

Ken Martin's Walker Pharmacy

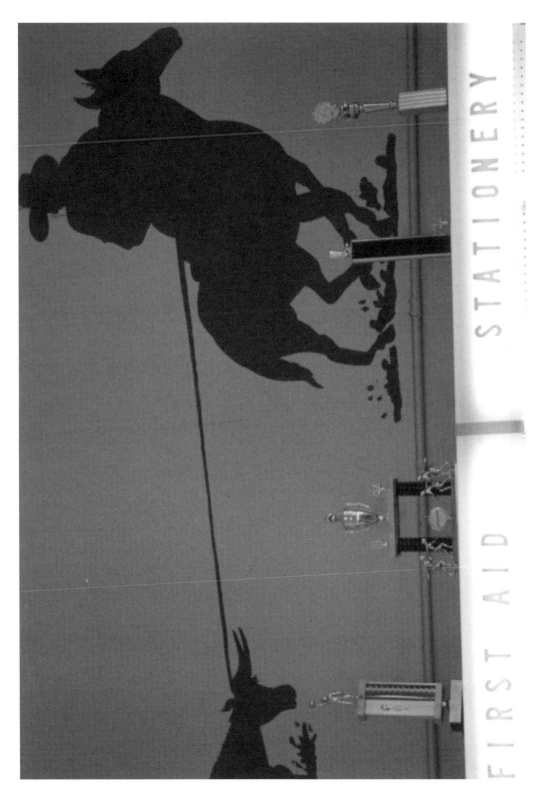

STATIONERY

FIRST AID

Ken Martin's Walker Pharmacy

29

DEE'S PLACE

Relying once again on Lady Luck, we left Madisonville, steered the car north on Interstate 45, and wandered through several towns before we arrived in Corsicana. We traveled slowly down North Beaton, a street paved with red bricks and lined with stately stone buildings. About midway down the street, Dee's Place—a modest-looking corner drugstore—popped into view and lured us in to check it out.

I gazed through the store's open doors and saw a long counter fronting a soda fountain. Inside, the first noticeable feature I spotted was the extensive collection of Dr Pepper items that filled the counter space in the fountain area, the shelves on the back wall, and the display cases scattered about the store. The room brimmed with glass cabinets full of historical Corsicana memorabilia, old candy jars, magazine racks, and sundry collectibles.

I selected one of the eight barstools at the counter and waited for the man with the jovial demeanor to take my soda order, Dr Pepper, of course. Then I watched as he used the old syrup dispensers to hand mix the drink, and I asked if the syrup canisters were originals. He replied, "Sure are. I wouldn't have it any other way." And when I requested to speak with the owner, he announced, "That'd be me, Dee Hawkinson."

Dee dove immediately into the store's background. He pointed out that the counter's base was original, but the old marble top had been replaced in the 1950s with the yellow Formica one. He explained that when the old chrome soda holders were replaced with fountain glasses, too many of the glasses broke against the unyielding marble. Then when age cracks began to show up in the old marble, the slab's beauty became marred, thus the Formica top.

Dee leaned over the counter and pointed out that the barstools were still bolted to the turn-of-the-century, flowered tile floor. He expressed his hopes to restore the place as close to its earliest condition as possible. First, he wants to remove the low ceiling that was installed in the 1950s because it obscures the old tin ceiling. After that he wants to remove the punch boards, also from the fifties, because they hide the antique mirrors. And finally he dreams of replacing the booths that were put in during World War II with some authentic 1900 ice cream tables.

At that moment, a young boy ran into the store and straight over to Dee, who immediately swooped the tot into his arms and hugged him. When Dee's son finally wriggled free he made himself at home amid the shelves of comic books and toys. As if his son had reminded him of something important, Dee turned back to our conversation and admitted that he loves summer best because it's when kids ride their bicycles to his place to drink sodas and lace the room with youthful laughter.

Dee's Place

One of the elderly men sitting in a booth overheard Dee's last statement and added, "I remember when we were kids and used to come in here. Why, back then a double dip of ice cream only cost 5¢ and you could buy a banana split for 10¢." Shortly I found myself sitting with and listening to the stories of Don, Doug, and Walter, three native Corsicanians.

I learned that according to legend a Mr. Louis Hashop was headed for Mexia in 1905 to start his family business, but when he came upon a Y in the road at Richland he found a dead man hanging from a tree. Doug laughed and said that since Mr. Hashop's mule was stubborn it couldn't be coaxed to go past the lifeless figure, so Louis took another road. And that's how he came to start his fruit and pharmacy business in Corsicana. I scribbled a note in my journal about how mysteriously the phantom of destiny works and ultimately sends a ripple through all that a person does in life.

Dee explained how Mr. Hashop had built the original store at another site in 1905 then in 1925 moved the business to the present location. Mr. Hashop ran the place for sixty-three years until his death in 1968, and at that time his son Will stepped in to continue the family legacy. Dee bought into the business in 1981, and later in 1990 he took over completely after Will retired.

All four men then exchanged thoughts about the 1960s and 1970s when shopping areas cropped up near the Interstate and changed life as they knew it. Walter pointed out that the strip malls pulled people away from downtown and caused the fountain business to decline. And Don added, "The saddest change is that too many of the old regulars are no longer with us."

Moved by this last statement, Dee looked over at the counter and recalled the old days when every afternoon around 5 o'clock the store would be crowded with customers, then he noted that now at that same hour of the day there are usually only five or six patrons in the store.

Dee then flashed his Cheshire grin and avowed, "But I know they'll come back. This is a good place and people need it. So I plan to keep it open!"

Dee's Place
125 N. Beaton
Corsicana, TX 75110
(903) 874-5891

Sonny Bryan's Smokehouse

SONNY BRYAN'S SMOKEHOUSE

Having idled our way up Interstate 45 from the town of Corsicana, the Dallas metropolitan nightlife hit us square in the face. Not ones to pass up a chance to mingle with the masses, we enjoyed a dinner and some music in the Deep Ellum area. The next morning we were intent on finding Sonny Bryan's Smokehouse, the barbecue place we had heard about, so we headed straight for its location on Inwood.

The black-top parking lot surrounded the small building beside which a cluster of picnic tables were set up. The place appeared empty, so I checked the time and realized it was only 9:55 in the morning. The wait proved a short one as it was only a couple of minutes before the front door opened.

Stepping in upon a concrete floor, I found myself in a small, rectangular-shaped room. To the right were the barbecue pits, the kitchen area, and the counter over which customers placed and picked up orders. Immediately to the left was an open-frame service counter that halved the room. Barbecue sauce, condiments, utensils, and napkins filled every inch of the counter. Beyond that open-framed divider was the dining area with benches that ran the full length of each wall. Twenty-four old school desk arms attached to the benches' backs offered side-by-side dining. Paned windows surrounded the section. The room felt cozy.

I was one of the first customers, but almost immediately people began filling the place. They ordered. They waited. The telephone rang continuously. One waitress busied herself with the pick-up orders. And in spite of the absence of air conditioning, no one appeared bothered by the ever increasing warmth of the room.

At 10:15 A.M., the place held nine diners from all walks of life: a business man and woman, a blue collar worker, an older couple, two young adults, the photographer, and myself. A mere five minutes later, six people stood in line to pick up orders, the phone had rung approximately twelve times, and thirteen happy campers now sat at the desk-like tables and ate barbecue sandwiches. It didn't matter to any of us that we dined within inches of one another.

While I ate in silence, I observed the man who appeared solely responsible for serving the food, so I decided to go over to get a closer look at him. His face cracked with canyons of character lines that encircled sparkling eyes and an ever-present grin. Since everyone seemed to know him by name, I introduced myself and watched as Charlie Riddle traversed the distance between the smoke pits and cutting boards. (Mr. Riddle has since passed away.)

Before long Charlie called for a worker to continue cutting the meat, and he came from behind the counter to talk with me. His energy brought personality to the place.

Sonny Bryan's Smokehouse

In quick, staccato sentences Charlie chronicled the history of Sonny Bryan's Smokehouse. In 1910 Elijah Bryan moved to Dallas from Tennessee and opened the first Bryan's Barbecue. Then, in 1935, his son William Jennings Bryan, nicknamed "Red" for his hair color, opened his own restaurant at another location. Red's son, Sonny, started helping out at the diner when he was eight years old, and many years later Sonny kept the family business going when he opened his own place on February 10, 1958. Since Sonny's death in 1989, a group of investors along with Michael LeMaster, the current manager, are ensuring that the legend of Sonny Bryan's Smokehouse lives on.

Charlie, who had cooked and managed the place since 1971, talked of others who had been with the business even longer than he. Several of the employees represented a span of up to thirty-eight years of service, and one employee worked for Red and Sonny for about fifty years.

With a sense of pride he explained that when the barbecue place is the busiest every inside table and outside picnic table will be filled. Then he grinned and added, "Don't be surprised to see people sitting on their Cadillacs, Mercedes, and Jaguars enjoying one of our mouth-watering sandwiches."

The last words Charlie shared with me were, "You be sure to stop back by the next time you're in Dallas. We always keep the fires burning."

Sonny Bryan's Smokehouse
2202 Inwood
Dallas, TX 75235
(214) 357-7120

Sonny Bryan's Smokehouse

Sonny Bryan's Smokehouse

Highland Park Pharmacy

HIGHLAND PARK PHARMACY

We headed to a local pharmacy we had heard about. The drive through the Dallas streets eventually led to the corner of Travis and Knox where in all its grandeur loomed a two-story building that housed the legendary Highland Park Pharmacy.

The interior was splendid. To the left and stretching the entire length of the spacious store stood a polished, deeply hued wooden counter. The mirrors behind it reflected contented customers at fifteen of the barstools. The remaining five stools were unoccupied. I sat at the counter's curved end located near the front of the store and watched the crowd of teenagers and adults talk with one another. Giddy gab sessions dovetailed with calm conversations.

The waitresses moved like mother finches as they flitted about filling orders. One waitress, a svelte blonde with a bubbly personality, captured my attention. With a sudden twist of her head she fixed her bright blue eyes on me and seemingly winged my way.

"What can I get you?" she chirped as she unhooked the pencil from the pin on her blouse. "One of our great shakes?" she asked. Following her lead, I ordered a shake and added a grilled cheese sandwich. "With or without lettuce?" she asked. "Without," I replied.

She turned and warbled to the cook at the far end, "Give me an American, hold the hay, and cremate it." I glanced around, a bit amused that nobody else seemed to take special interest in this novel lingo. While I waited, this lively lady cleaned dishes, took orders, mixed more shakes, and darted up and down behind the counter.

And all the while she flashed her bright smile.

A newspaper article that had been enlarged and framed hung on the side wall and caught my attention. As I studied it, I realized that the lady pictured in the article was the perky waitress who had just taken my order. I scooted over a couple of stools to read the story.

I learned that our waitress, Sarah Rogers, had begun her reign as the fountain queen on March 10, 1957. (Sarah has since passed away.) Next to the article about Sarah hung another story about Charlie Day, none other than the acclaimed fountain king who, in 1925 at age sixteen, had begun working at Highland Park Pharmacy and became the fountain manager four short years later.

Apparently it was Day who had concocted the unique fountain lingo. This former fun-loving manager had dubbed a pimento cheese sandwich a "Palm Beach," a ham salad sandwich without lettuce a "mince and hold the hay," and if a customer wanted either one grilled, Day would add the phrase "cremate it."

Years later Mr. Day became the owner and carried out that role for fifty or so years. For longer than twenty years Charlie and Sarah obviously had combined their personalities to contribute to the fountain's success and character.

As I continued to read about the pharmacy's history, I backtracked a bit to piece together further details of its legacy. It had originated in 1912 under the ownership of H. S. Forman of Tyler and at that time was housed in a site across the street from the present location. In the early 1920s, Mr. Forman moved the business to the present site and ran the business for twenty-eight years. Upon his retirement in 1940, he sold the place to four of his employees. They ran the pharmacy as a joint venture until 1973 when Thell Bowlin, who has continued to preserve the pharmacy's long-standing character, became the sole owner.

I then turned my attention back to the fountain when Sarah slid my order onto the counter. "Go ahead, try the shake," she urged. I did, and upon seeing my immediate satisfaction, she turned to her other customers. I slurped. I stuffed my face. And I smiled.

Later Sarah shared that the one thing she had treasured over the years was that many of the daughters of regular customers had become her namesakes. A lady sitting nearby then politely joined the conversation and recounted her own childhood days when she and her mother frequented the fountain not only to savor a shake but also to visit with Sarah. This woman pointed to her young daughter sitting like a little princess on the stool next to her and crooned, "I'd like you meet MY Sarah." It felt like a perfect ending to a fairy tale story.

All in all, I realized there are many reasons Highland Park Pharmacy customers return again and again. Not only is the food delicious, the lingo entertaining, and the building elegant, but the service is warm and the staff is personable.

Highland Park Pharmacy
3229 Knox
Dallas, TX 75205
(214) 521-2126

Highland Park Pharmacy

Hut's Hamburgers

HUT'S HAMBURGERS

A man dressed in all black and wearing sunglasses strolled out of the white stucco building with royal blue trim that stands on Sixth Street in Austin. As he passed by us, he smiled and nodded. Two young women dashed out of the place, and they too greeted us as they went on their way. And just as I pulled back the door, a young child chirped, "Come on in." She turned to her mother and giggled. I took all of these brushes with congeniality as a good sign and guessed that Hut's Hamburgers must be a place where friendly, happy people dine.

Once inside the restaurant, I became a mere minnow in a pond of Friday night diners waiting for a table. Looking around, I noticed that no one appeared edgy and no one complained. A few people held closet conversations, some checked out the framed pictures and articles on the walls, and others sat with their noses to the newspapers. I placed my name on the wait list then sidled over to the counter. No luck. Patrons had staked claim to all thirteen barstools.

Luckily, ten minutes later I was being led across the black-and-red tiled floor, past black-and-red tables and booths, and over to the raised dining area at the back of the restaurant. The walls and ceiling were decorated with sports pennants, old newspaper articles, black-and-white photos, and metal signs. No radio or television blared, and even though the place was packed, there was a distinct feeling of uncrowdedness.

I was seated at a table near a mural of Dagwood of comic strip fame painted on the back wall that proclaimed Homer "Hut" Hutson's restaurant to be the "Home of the Dag Burger." Before long I began to read the diner's history printed on the menu, which was tucked between the napkin dispenser and the catsup bottle. I soon learned that Hut's Hamburgers was originally built on South Congress in late 1939. In 1950 it was moved twice, once to another Sixth Street location and ten years later to its present site.

The waitress took my order, and when she turned I noticed the back of her T-shirt touted the message, "God Bless Hut's." I asked her about the saying when she came back with my drink, and she instantly launched into the explanation.

After the current owners, Mike Hutchinson and Chuck Gist, bought the business in 1981, Austin experienced a flood. Not just a little flood but a flood that reached toad-choker levels. Shoal Creek, which runs beside the restaurant, leaped over its banks and wreaked havoc by either washing away or causing severe damage to many of the businesses in its path. Miraculously Hut's took in only one foot of water, and when it was all over someone commented that "God must have blessed Hut's" and saved it from the throes of disaster. Thus, the saying.

Hut's Hamburgers

I finished the meal, noticed an opening at the bar, and since I was not quite ready to leave sat down on one of the stools. Within seconds I found myself speaking with the bartender, Steve Price, who not only has worked at Hut's for the past five years but has been coming into the diner since his days at the University of Texas during the 1960s. As Steve juggled his attention amongst the counter customers, I took note of the surrounding decor.

On the bar's overhang a collection of license plates lined the underside while artistic black-and-white photos from "Chuck's Gallery" adorned the front. Behind the black Formica counter, I observed a large deer head with a cigar in its mouth, a gold ball clock, and an old soda dispenser. To the left, a giant buffalo head that wore a baseball cap presided over customers sitting in a semiprivate alcove.

When Steve had time to visit with me, he told stories about the days when the house band, Tex Thomas and the Dangling Wranglers, had played weekly. Tex would preach as he played, so many popular local and regional musicians claimed they were "going to church at Hut's on Sunday" when they came to enjoy the music. Even though Hut's doesn't offer live music today, Steve confirmed that many well-known musicians still make the diner a regular stop.

Looking around, I could easily understand why this eclectic restaurant pulled in patrons from all walks of life. I also left with a better understanding as to why customers would wait patiently for a table on a busy Friday night. I scribbled into my journal, "Homer 'Hut' Hutson sure knew what he was doing when he opened his restaurant back in 1939!"

Hut's Hamburgers
807 W. 6th Street
Austin, TX 78701
(512) 472-0693

Hut's Hamburgers

Dirty Martin's Place

DIRTY MARTIN'S PLACE

A customer who overheard our conversation with the bartender at an Austin diner encouraged us to check out another popular burger joint in the capital city. Late in the evening, around 10:00 P.M., we got in the car and cruised down Lavaca and Guadalupe. Not long into the evening's excursion we spotted Dirty Martin's Place, a quaint, two-story white building.

I parked out front under a tall carport. As I walked to the restaurant, a young woman who sat at a table on the front porch nodded a hello. Her golden Labrador lay curled faithfully at her feet. Then I stepped through the diner's door.

To the right, four booths lined the front wall and ran parallel to an orange Formica counter, which offered seven tall orange-and-chrome pedestal barstools. Behind the counter an open-air grill allowed customers to savor the varied culinary aromas as they watched the cook perform his artistry. Along the left side of the room, a short hallway lined with photos and articles about Texans and the University of Texas led to yet another dining area. This room also offered customers a choice of tables and a counter, but since there was no grill in the section, I headed back to the front room.

Soon I met the cashier, Margie Alexander, and learned she had worked at Dirty's for twenty-one years along with her mom, Miss Liz, who had served as manager of Dirty's for quite a while. When I appeared impressed by their lengthy work records, Margie cocked her head ever so slightly and added that the daytime cook, Wesley, had them both beat. He had started working at Dirty's in 1955.

After placing an order, I settled back to watch the night cook work steadily and unhurriedly, a pace governed by the late hour and the thin crowd. Because things moved slowly, Margie had time to talk with me about Dirty's history.

It all started with John Martin in 1926. At that time, he installed a gas station that was separated from the diner he built. Since Mr. Martin's restaurant only had a dirt floor it was dubbed "Dirty" Martin's Place by the first set of regular customers.

In 1941 Stuart Nemir became the owner, and in 1954 he sold it to Cecil Pickens, who ran the place for thirty-five years. It was under Cecil's management in the 1950s that the original diner's dirt floor was replaced with concrete. Then in the 1960s, the gas station was remodeled as a dining area and connected to the restaurant, thereby almost doubling Dirty Martin's Place.

While I listened, a man walked in and Margie introduced Mark Nemir, who had bought the business in 1989. Taking a brief moment out of his busy schedule, he reminisced about the time he had spent at the restaurant when his grandfather, Stuart Nemir, had owned it. He shared that it had always been a dream of his to follow in his grandfather's footsteps.

Dirty Martin's Place

As he left, he reminded Margie to tell me about the sign on the building's front wall which reads, "For Curb Service Turn on Headlights." Margie explained that the sign meant just what it says. All a customer has to do is park under the carport, turn on the car's headlights, wait patiently, and eventually someone will be out to take their order. "Nice touch," I thought to myself.

When Margie left to wait on a new customer, I turned my attention to the quaint alliance of diners. At the counter two fresh-eyed coeds shared a plate heaped with fried onion rings. In a booth directly behind me, a family of four ate hamburgers and french fries while sloshing down milkshakes. Two booths away, five teenagers, each with multi-colored hair, sipped coffee and shared philosophical views about life. At the register, an older gentleman in a plaid shirt, blue jeans, and a large white cowboy hat waited to pay his tab. He chewed on a toothpick.

Before leaving, I recorded a few notes about this Austin hot spot and its diversity of diners, its mouth-watering food, and its good service. And then I made a note to return one evening, park under the carport, turn on the headlights, and wait.

Dirty Martin's Place
2808 Guadalupe
Austin, TX 78705
(512) 477-3173

Dirty Martin's Place

OLD TIMES BAR & GRILL

After leaving Austin's hectic pace, heading north on Interstate 35, and turning onto U.S. 79, everything changed. Crowded buildings were replaced with sprawling farmland. Bumper-to-bumper traffic jams were replaced with the occasional passing pickup truck. And it was in this sedate, pictorial setting that we found the next prospect. At the intersection of FM 973 and 1660, better known as Rice's Crossing, two older buildings stood on opposite corners. One was a general store; the other, a bar and grill. Since it was near lunchtime, we opted for the grill.

The small red-and-white wooden building with an old bench on the front porch was simple in design, and a sign beside the front door that read, "Open at 10 or Thereabout," indicated a place where the owners didn't let life push them to hurry.

Stepping inside, I noticed the high-gloss hardwood floor. An old jukebox placed against the left wall sat mute. A breeze blew gently through the long front room and on into the larger back room. To the right was a short wooden counter with six freestanding barstools. Two men lolled over their beer and chatted with the pretty, blond-haired Georgia (Georgy) McCurry, who stood behind the counter.

With a rosy, flushed face she asked, "What can I get you?" I ordered and she disappeared into the kitchen where she began to open jars, unwrap food, and jingle utensils. Amidst it all, the aroma of sizzling ground beef and onions permeated the place. The men continued to talk, so I continued to walk around.

The restaurant felt like an archive. Antique metal and neon signs covered the walls, and strings of decorative lights enhanced the decor. Photos of family, customers, and celebrities hung everywhere. Faded newspaper articles about the business and its owners were sprinkled amongst the photographs. And I realized that many of these snapshots highlighted the gregarious woman who had greeted me when I entered.

Driven by curiosity, I peeked through the side screen door that led outside to a neatly mowed area with five picnic tables and benches. The community-style courtyard was graced by two chinaberry trees that sweetened the air with their blooms' lilac scent. A large work barn stood in the not-so-far distance, and cattle grazed lazily in a field across the street.

Returning to the counter, I started a conversation with Georgy, and between orders she talked about her family's business. She explained that she is the daughter of the original owners and that now she helps her own daughter, Marcia (Marcy) Teague, with the responsibilities. Needing only a slight urging, Georgy soon pulled up a stool to continue her tales.

Her papa and mama, Joe and Francis Janosec, bought this property back in 1935 from a Mr. Avery. At that time Joe turned

Old Times Bar & Grill

an existing building used for repairing Model T Fords into a mill for grinding feed and cornmeal for local farmers. He provided that service from around 1935 until 1939, and later he built the front portion of the bar and grill and opened his new business, Joe's Place. The counter was built at that time, but Georgy was quick to explain that it had been covered with this new wooden countertop when a local musical celebrity used the grill and counter in one of his films. The family has chosen to leave the remodeled counter in place as a conversation piece.

Georgy went on to explain that in 1941 Joe added the back room and put in a pool table, slot machines (which have long been taken out), and dining tables for the busloads of World War II soldiers who were stationed at Camp Swift in Bastrop. He and Mama Janosec ran the business until his death in 1977. After that Mrs. Janosec carried on the family legacy for a while, making only one slight change when she renamed the place Mama Joe's.

When Georgy's mother died in 1982, the family decided to lease the business, and for years it passed through the hands of several managers who ran it under yet another new name, Mom's Place.

Then Georgy's daughter, Marcy, stepped in to run the family business. Although the name has been changed to the Old Times Bar & Grill, Mama Janosec's spirit still lives on. Following her good example, Marcy and Georgy still provide tasty food, reasonable prices, and a friendly place where families can bring their children.

When I asked Georgy if they had ever considered selling the family business, she quickly responded, "Why no, we never would have sold it off. It's part of our heritage."

Old Times Bar & Grill
15218 FM 1660
Taylor, TX 76574
(512) 365-9534

Old Times Bar & Grill

Old Times Bar & Grill

Cele General Store

CELE GENERAL STORE

We didn't have to continue the trek too far outside Austin's city limits to experience the unruffled countryside. The zig-zagging along farm and county roads between Hutto and Taylor proved to be calming, so we rolled down the car windows and tasted the spicy air. It was on one of the many "zigs" of the "zagging" that we saw a structure weathered by the fingers of time. The almost unreadable lettering on the building announced the Cele General Store.

I left the bright out-of-doors and stepped inside to find a room awash in twilight. The afternoon sun's illuminations sifted in through the two front windows and screen door, and its gauzy rays flirted with the luster from the few lamps scattered about. The lanky man standing behind the counter nodded, barely breaking stride in his conversation with a customer who lounged on one of the five barstools.

Walking past them, I took a seat midway down the counter. I noted my entrance had barely made a dent in the customer count yet the room felt lively. Soon, the tall man stood before me and took my order. He automatically reached into the cooler, pulled out a beer, and placed it down onto the counter. But before he could walk back over to his pal, I asked him a few simple questions; I soon found myself enamored by the gentle yet intense manner in which he answered each one.

Marvin Weiss exhibited a strong sense of self. As he talked about the store's history, he walked over to a massive antique floor safe which had once been used by an insurance company in nearby Taylor. He lugged open the safe's leaden door and mentioned that this piece had been in this store long before he and his wife, Marilyn, had bought the business.

While rustling through some of the safe's papers, he recalled the store's saga. The building was built by Mr. Moreland in 1891 and named the Richland Saloon; however, years later Mr. Moreland lost the business. Then some time before 1900, Gus Wendland bought the place only to also lose it around 1917. The store remained closed until 1933 when Mr. Ewald Weiss (no kin to Marvin) bought it. It was from Ewald that Marvin and Marilyn purchased the place in 1951. He handed a small bundle of old newspaper and ledger pages to me, so I scanned them.

As he continued his stories, he ran his tanned farmer's hands along the smooth walnut counter and recounted how this beautiful piece of furniture had been moved out of a Pflugerville saloon and placed in the store by Mr. Wendland. That dated the counter back about ninety years. He pointed to a quarter embedded into the counter's top and offered a side tale. (If you make it to the store, be sure to ask Marvin about it.)

When Marvin's wife, Marilyn, came out of an office to talk to him, I took the time to look around. I gazed through the grayish

Cele General Store

glint cast into the room and found a peacefulness in its illuminance. I noticed tiny specks of dust being tossed about by the old ceiling fan that had once been used in an old Pflugerville parsonage. The slow, perpetual evolutions of the fan's blades harmonized rhythmically with the Weiss' whispers. There was a sanctity in these shushing sounds as I sat inside my reflective cocoon.

At the counter's end stood an old ice cream freezer. And once again, I spotted the ubiquitous mounted deer heads and antlers I had seen in so many Texas hot spots. Tools and farm implements dotted the walls. Old cotton-picking sacks were strung neatly along a makeshift clothesline. An original photo of the Richland Saloon hung above the back bar. Shelves held grocery and hardware items.

Then I spied an antique nail bin and above it, a stool that hung from the rafters. As I walked up closer to inspect it, Marilyn sauntered up behind me and talked about the handful of film companies that had shot movie scenes in the store. She mentioned the celebrities with whom they had rubbed elbows then pointed at the stool and made note of the star's autograph on its seat. (If you make it to Cele, be sure and check out this stool.)

We walked to the end of the counter and I mentioned to Marilyn that I had heard from folks in Taylor that the Weiss' were famous for their barbecue. Marvin chimed in at that point and said, "I don't know if you'd say we're famous, but we sure sell a lot of it."

Marilyn explained that they serve only on Friday and Saturday nights because their neighbors and friends are too busy with dawn-to-dusk farming duties during the week. The Weisses keep it simple, serving only meats and drinks. The diners, who eat on paper plates and often bring their own side dishes, pack the place every weekend and fill the room with casual camaraderie.

Marvin then checked his watch and reported he had to go spread some fertilizer, so I reluctantly gathered my things. Before I left, Marvin commented, "You know, it's strange. Today I'm seeing more country folk who go to town for their entertainment, and more and more town folk who come to the country for theirs."

Cele General Store
18726 Cameron Road
Manor, TX 78653
(512) 251-3562

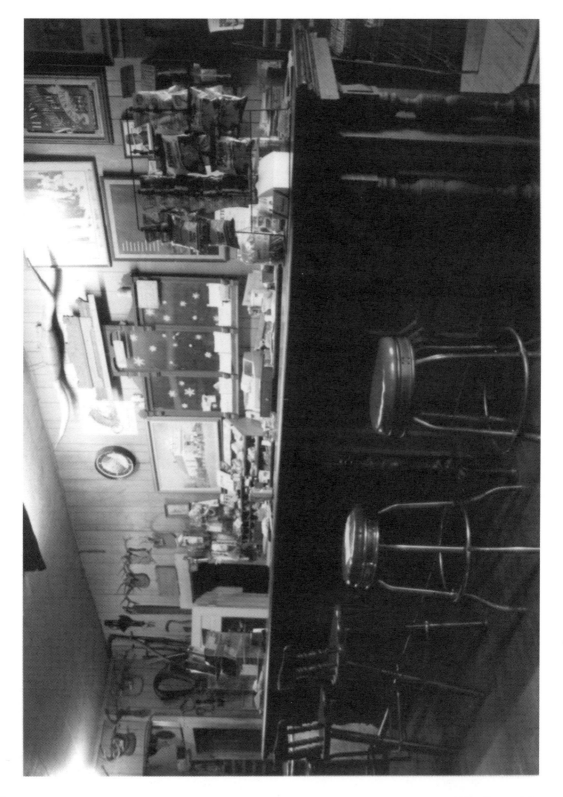

Cele General Store

Tex Miller's

TEX MILLER'S

Yesterday afternoon we meandered through the country before turning onto Texas Highway 36, passing through Caldwell, and heading over to Cameron. We checked out the town square, but things didn't look too promising, so a survey of the side roads was necessary. In five minutes we hit pay dirt. Tucked away on Fannin Street we found a simple red-and-white diner with a grill and counter, and although the place was closed, it held promise for a return visit.

Around 10:35 A.M. the next morning I found Tex Miller's porch fan on and the front door open, so I went in. The woman behind the grill offered a quick greeting and asked, "What can I get you?" I ordered the usual, a jalapeño burger and a cola. She plopped the ball of fresh ground beef onto the freestanding grill, picked up a well-worn cement trowel, and pressed the meat onto the hot grill. Within minutes she handed the burger to me and motioned to the jars of condiments on the small service counter.

I took the first bite, the second, the third, . . . and wanted more. As I ate, in walked a local. "Hi, Johnny." "Hi, Sandy. Two, please." Simple as that. He entered. Hello's were exchanged. He didn't tell her what he wanted; she just knew. He sat down. She cooked. She served. He ate. He paid. Another customer entered. "Hi, Dennis." "Hi, Sandy." And there you have it, a true Tex Miller's experience.

Tex Miller's is a simple place. It offers a simple menu. And it has simply scrumptious food. By 11:25 A.M. all eleven of the seats that run along the wall opposite the grill were taken. Soft drinks, bags of chips, and newspapers rested on old wooden school desk arms attached to the back of the two benches that provided seating. People carried on pocket conversations with one another. Sandy chatted with everybody as she faced her clientele like a lone cook at her island of a grill.

She never got flustered. She never wrote down an order. And better yet, she never got an order wrong. There was a cadence, a rhythm to the entire scene as it was played out.

All of the orders came wrapped in paper. There were no plates, no silverware, no glassware. We got the soft drinks or milk out of the cooler ourselves and placed the empty bottles in the rack or the empty cartons in the trash can. Everyone cleaned up after themselves.

Once things died down I talked to the cook, Sandy Terry, and learned she had owned the business since 1989. Between 1986 and 1989, Reggie Hayes and his wife ran it, and before that George "Tex" Miller owned and ran the business.

Tex opened the diner in 1936 at a site around the corner from its present location. Then in 1937 he built the present small building to begin his forty-nine years of dedicated service. From the 1930s through the 1950s, when the business saw its heyday, Tex started working at four or five in

Tex Miller's

the morning and wouldn't leave until around midnight. That was before television when people flocked to the downtown stores for fellowship and the picture shows for entertainment, and it was common knowledge that Tex Miller's diner was a hot spot for a good burger, a cold drink, and some sweet socializing.

Sandy recalled the old-timers' stories about lunch lines stretching down the sidewalk and around the corner, and how Tex used to pipe music outside for their enjoyment. He even hired teenagers to carhop all the way to the courthouse in order to keep his customers happy.

She said Tex was always gregarious and accommodating except during the city's centennial celebration when he and some hired help cooked up and served over six hundred hamburgers in two hours. That day the customers had no choice—they got their burgers fixed one way or not at all.

Much about the business remains the same. There is the same old Superior refrigerator, the same old recipe for chili dogs, and the same old unairconditioned building. Yet, as with all things, change happens.

Sandy said she has a steady business but nothing like Mr. Miller's during the early days. She added, "People just don't come downtown to shop and eat like they used to since so many of the businesses have moved toward the main highway."

Although the counter isn't one at which people can sit, it is one over which conversation travels, over which good food is served, and over which simplicity is still stressed. I stayed until Sandy cleaned up and then walked out with her.

As she turned off the front porch ceiling fan and closed the door, she said, "Everyone knew that Mr. Miller's place was open for business when the fan was on and the door was open, and some things just shouldn't be changed!"

Tex Miller's
104 N. Fannin
Cameron, TX 76520
(254) 697-4302

Tex Miller's

Tex Miller's

Girvin Social Club

GIRVIN SOCIAL CLUB

The trek through West Texas was an eye-opener. As we played leapfrog from town to town along Interstate 10, panoramic vistas engulfed us. We stopped to visit two friends who lived in Fort Stockton, and they insisted that we go to Girvin and take a gander at the old saloon run by a lady and her dog. Intrigued, we set out.

The snake-like sojourn through the hypnotic landscape ended at the crossroads of U.S. 67 and FM 11. Squinting my eyes through the swirling dust kicked up by the car, I saw a sign on one of the two existing buildings that read, Girvin Social Club. We had a good feeling about this one.

As I approached the building on the left, a ghostly West Texas wind set the screen door to bouncing. I bounded up the front steps and peeked in, but no one was in sight. I glanced over at the other building, but it too appeared closed up.

I hesitated then turned to leave but was immediately greeted by a horn blast from the truck that whipped into the lot. Out hopped a man and a woman. "Mildred'll be here sooner or later. Come on in," hollered the man.

I followed, as did Mark, and they introduced themselves as Hope and Larry. Hope sat at one of the four short stools in front of the small, pockmarked cedar bar. She let the table fan sitting atop the counter cool her. Larry walked to the refrigerator, looked inside, then announced, "Mildred's out of beer, but I've got some ice-cold ones out in the truck. You're more than welcome to a couple." I nodded in acceptance and found a place to sit at one of the six cable spool tables.

For the sake of capturing some initial observations, I opened my journal and began sketching and scribbling. Two fans hanging from the tin ceiling did little to create a breeze in the toasty room. A mishmash of items—painted cow skulls, faded signs, and rusty horseshoes—were nailed on the walls. Old school bus benches placed along the room's edge provided ample seating. An old powder bomb, a reminder of military days gone by, rested in the far corner across from the television set that stood beside a wood-burning stove. A daytime soap opera flickered on the screen. Waves of air drifted through the front door and blew hot breath across our faces as we took deliberate draughts of our beers and continued to chitchat.

The side door swung open and in strolled Mildred Helmers and her dog, Freckles. This tall, slender lady moved fluidly as if she knew exactly where she was going and how fast she had to go to get there. Wisps of short, baby-fine hair feathered about her head to frame a face graced with character lines. As she cut her crystal blue eyes at me, she perched on a stool behind the counter and lit a cigarette. Larry

introduced Mildred and the party picked up from there.

Within seconds our conversations ran from fishing to snakes to big cities. We talked about the beauty of open spaces and the peacefulness of West Texas. And throughout it all, we were drawn into a single sphere. With this welcomed sense of comfort, I asked Mildred if she would share the Social Club's history.

She rose, went into the back room, and before long, reappeared with a copy of *National Geographic* dog-eared to an article on the Pecos River. She pointed to the two pictures of her place that had been included and smiled. Hope and Larry chimed in and said, "Guess you're in good company." I agreed.

Mildred sat back down, lit up another cigarette, and began the story of the social club. She first talked about "old" Girvin that once sat a mile off the road. It had its multifaceted start as an oil boomtown, a ranching center, and a railroad shipping point for livestock. However, it became a ghost town in the early 1930s when U.S. 67 was built a mile away from the old town. In 1955 Mildred and her husband moved the short distance to the main road, and three years later, in 1958, the Helmers opened the Girvin Social Club.

She reminisced about the days when they had parties and dances and the jukebox was always playing for the regulars. "But many of them have died," she said, quickly adding that since there are only three Girvinites left, most of her business comes from nearby towns. After she talked briefly about her husband's death in 1983, you could have heard a flea hop. We sat there enchanted by the quietness; its spell broken only by the serenading West Texas wind as it whispered through the room.

A feeling that I had just experienced a true Texas moment washed over me, so it felt appropriate to close the interview. As I walked down the front porch steps, I turned and took one last look in through the screen door to freeze frame a picture of this lady, her dog, and the Girvin Social Club.

Girvin Social Club
U.S. 67 & FM 11
Girvin, TX 79740
(915) 652-3016

Girvin Social Club

Henderson Collins Soda Fountain and Malt Shop

HENDERSON COLLINS SODA FOUNTAIN AND MALT SHOP

Following the stop in Girvin, we headed north on U.S. 385. Conversation was at a standstill as we both let our last visit lull our memories. Then after traveling across many more wide-open West Texas stretches, we finally hit the town of Odessa. Its roads offered a peaceful, easy drive, and it was along Grant Street that a bright red-and-yellow sign demanded my attention. The colorful sign heralded the Henderson Collins Soda Fountain and Malt Shop.

Slowing down the car to a crawl, I peered through the shop's open door and caught sight of a counter brimming with customers. Satisfied with this picture, I knew it was time to check this one out.

The store was long and narrow. Along the room's left side a well-worn, orange-and-white Formica counter stretched halfway down the building's length. Several children and adults sat at the counter eating their lunch while a petite woman conversed with them as she cooked.

I scanned the rest of the room. In the middle section stood eight booths, three of which were occupied with small gaggles of women. The right side of the room was taken up by an antique merchandise counter covered with old-fashioned calculators, typewriters, and cash registers. Directly behind this old counter were shelves filled with memorabilia. Toward the back of the building stood three more dining booths, an original telephone booth, and more partially filled shelves. It was if I had taken a huge step back in time.

While I looked at the items, a delicate voice crooned, "Can I get you something?"

I turned and there stood Pearl Collins drying her dainty hands on a dish towel. She wore a sheer blouse trimmed with lace and a white pleated skirt covered by a voile apron. Her ensemble was fashionably accessorized by a pearl necklace and pearl earrihgs. She was a poised picture of a proper Texas woman.

I took a seat near the other five customers who sat at the counter. I ordered and watched as Pearl prepared everything from scratch. All the while that she chopped, diced, and cooked, she caught up on the latest news with her friends, and I found myself increasingly intrigued with this woman.

Before long Pearl related the story of the soda fountain to me. Its history began as Henderson Drugs in 1906 in an old historical building located at 204 N. Grant. Then, in 1929, Mr. Henderson moved his store to a new location at 122 N. Grant; as business grew, he expanded and brought Pearl's husband, Jack Collins, into the venture in 1931. She reminisced about the 1940s during World War II when their store hours ran from five or six in the morning until midnight in order to provide a

Henderson Collins Soda Fountain and Malt Shop

gathering place for soldiers from nearby bases. Then after the war ended, they cut back on the hours.

That building burned in 1949, and afterward the two men took over the Fitz Pharmacy, at this present site, and they renamed the business Henderson Collins Pharmacy. Pearl placed a hand atop the counter in front of her and said, "I remember that this counter was already here when Jack moved in." Within eight years of that move, Jack Collins bought the business and—up until his death in 1994—worked alongside Pearl to secure the fountain's success.

She talked about how rich her life has been. She spoke lovingly about her late husband and how he was an old-fashioned druggist, a real jack-of-all-trades. Spurred by that memory, she reached behind her and took a photo of him washing dishes off the wall and handed it to me. Then she introduced me to her granddaughter, Lona, who works at the fountain alongside Pearl. The two smiled at each other.

After Jack's death, she decided to keep the business; however, she phased out the pharmaceutical lines and turned her attention strictly to the fountain. To give the place a personal touch, she renamed it Henderson Collins Soda Fountain and Malt Shop.

When she finished fixing some sandwiches, she served the customers sitting in a booth. As she stood beside them and conversed, I took one last look about the place. I studied the contented faces of those enjoying Pearl's food and company, and it made sense that she didn't have a fax machine, a copy machine, or even a modern touch-tone phone. Pearl Collins didn't need them to enjoy life.

Henderson Collins Soda
Fountain and Malt Shop
409 N. Grant
Odessa, TX 79761
(915) 332-4272

Henderson Collins Soda Fountain and Malt Shop

Green Hut Cafe

GREEN HUT CAFE

Continuing the journey northward, we made whistle stop after whistle stop looking for the next prize. This leg of the trip took us through Midland and then up State Highway 349 to Lamesa. A spin through downtown at around 10:30 in the morning wasn't proving very successful until we drove down Dallas Street. We slowly searched the few buildings in the area and I was about to suggest we move on to another city when we saw it, a sign spelling out the next possible adventure at the Green Hut Cafe.

Inside the cafe, I found a 1960s diner bustling in full force with a coffee break crowd. The decor offered a tile floor, a Formica counter with seven low barstools, and ten vinyl booths. Farmers drinking coffee and discussing the latest ranching and agricultural issues occupied several of the booths. A young woman behind the counter busily filled orders as I took a seat at one of the barstools. From where I sat, I was able to watch the cooks through a long serving window.

As the young waitress poured me a cup of coffee, she pointed out that the lady sitting down the way from me was the one I needed to talk with if I had questions. Within minutes I met Dorothy Hunter, who immediately made me feel at home as she suggested we move to a booth to be more comfortable while she shared what she knew about the Green Hut Cafe.

Dorothy said that although she was born in Marshall, Texas, she had basically grown up in Lamesa, and it had always been a dream of hers to own a cafe. She saw that dream fulfilled in June of 1993 when she started running the Green Hut.

She pointed out that her daughter Yolanda has worked at the cafe for over thirteen years and her brother Willie Butler has cooked at the diner for over twenty years. Her son Del Wayne Hunter serves as a business manager and works with Sam Brown, a relation of Dorothy's who has recently assumed the role of store manager.

As Dorothy offered this last piece of the puzzle, the young woman who toiled behind the counter came over, planted a big kiss on Dorothy's cheek, then asked if I was ready to order something to eat. That's when Dorothy, a proud grandmother, introduced me to her granddaughter, Keisha. I ordered, and Keisha returned to the counter.

Dorothy talked about the cafe's booming business. She shared that regulars, many of them local cotton farmers, not only keep the place hopping at breakfast, lunch, and dinner, but also stake out a booth every midmorning or midafternoon for their daily coffee breaks. According to Dorothy, one of the many perks of running this business is that the cafe patrons aren't rushing through life. And because of the customer's laid-back manners, Dorothy is able to flit from table to table and share in their conversations.

Green Hut Cafe

Dorothy talked about how the cafe had been repainted and some of the booths had been recovered around 1933, but other than those few changes it has remained pretty close to its original design. She commented on how the diner has "always been a great place to come to." Then she offered that if I wanted more information on the cafe, I needed to talk with Hap Bratcher. With that, she drew some directions to his office on a table napkin.

Following her little map, it was easy to find Mr. Bratcher's office. As soon as I entered the building, Carole Dyer, Mr. Bratcher's secretary, greeted me with a wide smile. And before I knew it, I found myself sitting with both Hap and Carole as they delved into the Green Hut Cafe's past.

Mr. Bratcher recalled that the original cafe was built by Clarence Newland in 1928 and stood on the east side of the downtown square. It was moved in the early 1940s to the south side of the square, and in 1943 Maurice and Beth Lamphere purchased the business.

Hap talked about the time when the cafe was connected to a hotel and bus station and its business thrived. However, he ruefully remembered that as downtown activity dwindled so did the cafe's business.

Mr. Bratcher then explained that when he bought the Plainsman Motel, which was located on Dallas Street, he also moved the Green Hut—which he had also purchased—to the site next to the motel. For a while, he successfully ran both businesses, but eventually he sold the motel only to retain ownership of the cafe. He has continued to rent or lease the cafe over the years to various people.

Just as Hap offered this last tidbit of the cafe's history, he received a call. Asking Carole to express my thanks to Mr. Bratcher, I then left the modest office feeling content that I had gathered some valuable pieces of the Green Hut Cafe's legacy and had experienced yet another pearl of Texas culture.

Green Hut Cafe
903 S. Dallas
Lamesa, TX 79331
(806) 872-7756

Green Hut Cafe

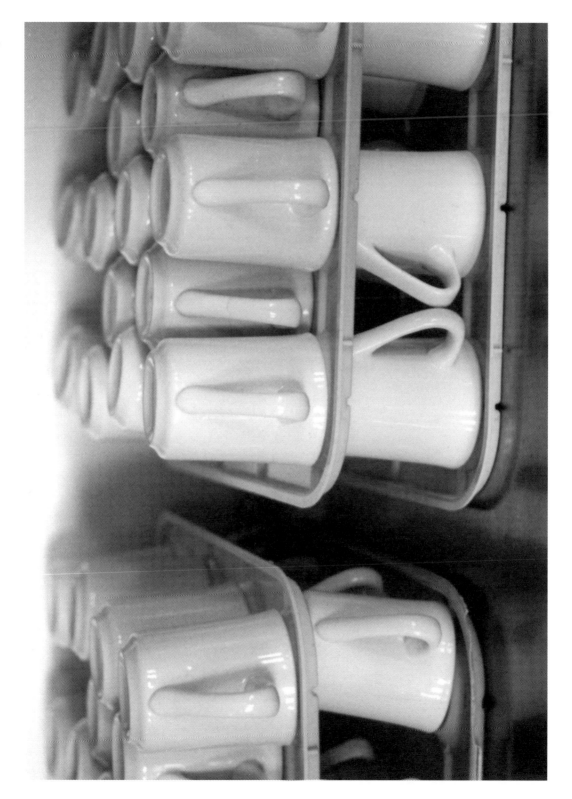

QUICK LUNCH

The close proximity of places in the Panhandle allowed for quicker connections in our dot-to-dot journey to the north along Interstate 87. As we ricocheted from town to town, We felt like a giant rubber band being pulled first eastward then westward. The crisscrossing pattern of the travels came to a halt only upon arrival in Plainview around 8:30 P.M. After searching street after street, a brightly lit cafe sign finally trumpeted the presence of the Quick Lunch.

Pulling up in front of the cafe, I got out to see if a counter might be housed in the darkened building. In the soft, blue-white of the car's headlights, my investigation was rewarded. Through the large plate-glass windows, I could see the shadowy outline of an enormous counter that filled the room's center and like a moonlit siren, beckoned a return the next day. So return I did.

Around 8:30 the next morning, I entered the cafe through one of the two doors positioned at either front corner. Standing just inside the entrance, I felt like a member of the late crowd. The cafe's twenty or so customers appeared to have long ago pushed back their breakfast dishes and now slowly drank refill after refill of coffee as they relaxed and visited.

The storefront windows that wrapped around one-third of the building created an open and inviting environment. Ten booths with worn green Formica tabletops and burnt orange vinyl seats lined both sides of the room. Six of the booths were occupied. Two tables, one small and the other large, were set up near the front and both burst at the seams with patrons.

Rounding out the picture was the counter, an enormous fixture that hugged the large grill and kitchen area. Orange pedestal bar stools complemented the counter's light green Formica top and stainless steel trim. A polished, stainless steel footrest snaked along the counter's entire base. This phenomenal piece of furniture, where only fifteen of the thirty-one barstools remained open, flaunted a formidable air.

Although I could have sat at the counter, I opted for a booth. Shortly after I scooted into the seat, the waitress took my order. As I waited, framed articles and pictures that lined the side and back walls of the cafe caught my attention. Seeing that many of them featured a particular movie and its celebrities, I made a note to ask about this.

The pancakes and coffee soon arrived, and in between bites and sips I observed the clientele. Again, as in so many other places in Texas, I realized that a neighborly ease existed amongst the diners. Before too long I enjoyed a visit with Juanita McElroy, who in an unhurried pace traced the history of the Quick Lunch back some seventy-odd years.

She recalled that the diner was built in 1921 by Charles Vanderpool but was not remodeled and enlarged until 1948. She pointed out that the old counter was

Quick Lunch

horseshoe-shaped; however, when a movie company used the cafe for several scenes in one of its films, the set crew reshaped the counter. It looked as if some large hands had gently inverted the front right corner of the counter to make room for dining tables. This piece of information also helped to explain the celebrity pictures and movie posters that hung about the place. (If you get a chance to stop at the Quick Lunch, check them out.)

Juanita explained that a Mr. Smelser had owned the building for a long time, and Milbra Harding had been its landlord. In 1997 Juanita, who had worked at Quick Lunch for thirty-one years, then bought the business.

Carolyn, Juanita's daughter, joined us and lovingly bragged on her mom. She first praised her mom's work ethic that is evidenced by the fact that Juanita—at the age of sixty-eight—still does the majority of cooking and works every Monday through Saturday. Carolyn added that her super-mom who "has never smoked or drank and who works because she loves it" opens the cafe at six in the morning and closes it at five in the afternoon. Juanita simply grinned at Carolyn's honeyed words, then went back to work.

Before long it was time to move on, so I thanked both hostesses and headed out the door, eager once again to roll like a tumbleweed across the wide-open spaces of the Texas Panhandle.

Quick Lunch
108 E. 7th
Plainview, TX 79072
(806) 296-9121

Quick Lunch

Quick Lunch

Cope's Coney Island

COPE'S CONEY ISLAND

With our questing spirit still in full force, we continued northward up Interstate 27. Once we passed through the little town of Happy, a sense that we were headed in the right direction tickled my fancy. So when we drove down 4th Avenue in Canyon and we noticed a small diner surrounded with cars parked willy-nilly, I chuckled. After reaching into the backseat and grabbing my notepad and pen, I felt giddy at the thought of a flock of cars about an eatery around lunchtime. Since we knew that could only be a good omen, I jotted down the restaurant's name, Cope's Coney Island.

When I entered the diner through its back door, lively voices and laughter revved up my spirits and the aroma of grilled food sent my taste buds into overdrive. Taking a quick scan, I noted that all twelve barstools at the raised counter were taken and the five booths across from them were filled. Then I felt my sense of humor slip a tad as the tables in the room's middle section didn't offer any seating options at this time either.

The two men and one woman who worked steadily behind the counter took order after order and balanced plates of food as they served the patrons. At the far end of the counter, one man orchestrated the food's preparation over an open grill.

Uncertain that a seat would open up soon, I had decided to leave when one of the waiters yelled for me to hang around. I did, and the wait turned out to be a short one. Nevertheless, in the tiny dash of time that I waited, I observed a den of diners where everyone appeared to delight in conversations over plates heaping with food. I felt my sense of humor being rekindled.

I asked the waitress if I could speak with the owner and was immediately introduced to Max Troub, one of the men working behind the counter. Max threw his dish towel in the sink and sidled over to shake my hand. As he directed me to an open booth, he promised that whenever things slowed down a bit, he would join me to talk about the Coney Island.

I ordered. I ate. And I waited. Finally, after forty-five minutes, Max could take a break, and with a rush he slid into the booth. He began chattering away about the relatively young history of this diner which began in 1987 when his good friend and business partner, Wayne Cope, decided to try his hand at the restaurant business. It seems that after Mr. Cope made this decision, he looked around Canyon and discovered there were plenty of hamburger, pizza, and steak places, but there was a need for a good hot dog diner. With that, Cope's Coney Island became a reality.

Max then launched into a spiel about Mr. Cope, who was born and reared only twelve miles south of Canyon. This West Texas farmer is apparently a man of many talents, and he has been an owner of many things: a service station, a trucking business, and now a diner.

Cope's Coney Island

Max, who has worked in feed grain trading as well as in cattle trading, rounds out the business venture. Together their efforts, experience, and expertise have proven successful.

Then Max explained the plans these two men have to slowly phase themselves out of the business as they look forward to retirement. He pointed to the grill cook. "That's my son, Craig, and I hope that one day he'll take over the business in order to keep it all in the family."

I learned that both Max and Wayne find great pleasure in meeting and chatting with the customers, who range from college students to longtime locals to summertime vacationers. I also learned that whether these customers are regulars who come by every working morning or visitors who happen by while on vacation, Max and Wayne make sure they all leave with full bellies and happy hearts.

Hearing a gusto of greetings, I turned and watched as a tall, self-assured-looking man entered through the back door. He returned the greetings, looked about, spotted Max, then took long strides toward us. Wayne Cope stopped briefly along the way to shake hands and share a word or two with customers.

Wayne and Max comfortably bantered about brotherly teasings and exchanges. While listening to them, I noted that their easy-going natures obviously dovetailed strong senses of humor with positive work attitudes to bring about a successful business partnership.

Cope's Coney Island
2201 4th Avenue
Canyon, TX 79015
(806) 655-1184

Cope's Coney Island

Cope's Coney Island

Hamlin Pharmacy

HAMLIN PHARMACY

Our southerly, streamlined jaunt along U.S. 59 and U.S. 77 exposed us to rambling coastal plains that invited the eyes and mind to wander. After we arrived in Corpus Christi, a walk along the seawall proved invigorating as gulf breezes blew ashore and the sun glowed rubescent against the ivory foam of the cresting waves.

The following morning we arose early and drove around the older section of town for several hours, but luck evaded us until we stopped at a shoreline restaurant and heard a waitress talk about a possible prospect further inland. That possibility proved to be a real gold mine when Hamlin Pharmacy, which stood at the corner of Weber and S. Staples, came into view.

The store's name, painted in bold turquoise, stood out against the wall's classic black-and-white checkerboard pattern. As I entered, Lady Fortune smiled softly. Over to the right I found not one horseshoe-shaped counter but rather two of them. They jutted out, provocative peninsulas at either end of the fountain area, and embraced three large booths.

Customers sat at both counters and in all three booths while a man with salt-and-pepper hair choreographed his comings and goings between the grill and the patrons. After selecting one of the short barstools, I ordered a shake and began to talk with this gregarious man, Jesse Lerma. Soon he explained that he had begun working at the drugstore when it opened in 1960 and for thirty-nine years has managed the fountain.

A steady flow of customers kept him darting hither and yon, and in between filling orders he took the time to listen to everyone's life sagas. When he had a free second, he introduced me to Karl Arnold, the owner and pharmacist. Instantly Karl's calm nature and sly sense of humor evoked images of the proverbial favorite 1960s dad. He spoke briefly about opening the pharmacy in 1960 and how he and his wife Joanne initially ran the place together. He explained that with the birth of each child, Joanne's time at the store lessened, eventually leading her to choose to be a stay-at-home mom.

As we talked, a pretty brunette walked over to him and he introduced Karen Nicholson, the youngest of his four children, who is the manager of the pharmacy. Karl left to fill some prescriptions, and Karen and I walked over to the counter.

She spoke of her grandmother, Ruth Arnold, who had worked at the drugstore until she was eighty-two years old. Lovingly Karen mentioned that it was Grandmother Ruth who was responsible for bringing her into the pharmacy when she was four years old and letting her have the run of the store. "That was when I actually fell in love with the pharmacy," Karen admitted.

Hamlin Pharmacy

When old enough to follow in her three brothers' footsteps, Karen began to work in the store part-time. After high school graduation she continued working at Hamlin's and has never stopped. Eagerly she shared her two favorite things about the fountain—its inviting atmosphere and the congenial customers. She added that many of those very same customers who hung out at the pharmacy as she grew up now bring their kids in to enjoy a slice from their past.

Looking around, I found it easy to see what Karen meant. Sitting in one booth was a grandmother with two grandchildren, and all three were enjoying large chocolate shakes. Across the room a mother and her teenage daughter shared a grilled sandwich, and at the far counter an elderly couple carried on a conversation with a young adult.

Jesse then joined us, and he and Karen recounted details about the regulars who have their own spots at the fountain. Jesse talked about the group of men who come in every morning, sit at the back counter to visit, and always leave a stool vacant for any member of their small clique who can't make it in that day.

Karen countered by adding that this group of men is rivaled only by the group of ladies who come in every weekday around three in the afternoon. They sit in their reserved booths and share their latest news. Both Jesse and Karen agreed that the people are the very foundation of the fountain.

Overhearing this last comment, Mr. Arnold recalled the 1970s when he almost took out the fountain, but then he mused that for some reason he didn't. Now he considers it a blessing that he has his own watering hole he can share with friends and out-of-towners. Before returning to work, he said simply that the pharmacy with its fountain is indeed "a home away from home."

Hamlin Pharmacy
3801 S. Staples
Corpus Christi, TX 78411
(512) 853-7303

Hamlin Pharmacy

Hamlin Pharmacy

Doll House Cafe

DOLL HOUSE CAFE

Mark and I left Corpus Christi so early that the only other souls moving about were the seagulls whose yawping and squawking stuffed the salty air with a cacophony fit only for a sailor. We ping-ponged about the region until we hit the jackpot in Cuero.

A trip down East Broadway gave rise to a homespun restaurant neatly painted white with green trim. From the looks of its exterior, we imagined an interior fraught with floral wallpaper, vases filled with pink-and-white carnations, and lovely ladies sharing their latest stories. But somehow the pickup trucks parked around the Doll House Cafe dispelled that image.

As I walked into the diner, I found myself face-to-face with a small counter that stretched to the left for about five or six feet then hooked into a slight curve, creating a gentle arc. Ranchers, many donning hats and smoking cigars, drank coffee as they spoke with one another. I scanned the room. There was no floral wallpaper, no vases filled with carnations, and at this moment, only two lovely ladies sharing the latest tidbits.

Some barstools stood vacant at the counter's curved end, so I grabbed one that would give me a vantage point either for talking with customers at the counter or for observing patrons at the tables. The waitress soon answered my question about the counter, explaining that it was built in 1959 to replace the old one that dated back to the 1930s.

I glanced around and noticed a hodgepodge of patrons. There were businessmen in dress suits, farmers in jumpsuits, and blue collar workers in jeans and work shirts. The two ladies wore flower-print dresses. And the ages of this community of customers ran a wide spectrum of years.

Most of the diners seemed to know one another, and all of them spoke to the sociable man behind the counter, Rollie Brantley. He shot the breeze with them about their families, the weather, and the latest city happenings. And he listened intently to what they had to say. His sense of humor bubbled up at just the right points.

Although the waitress took care of the orders, Rollie moved about behind the counter, being careful not to get in her way. He answered the phone, rang up bills, and talked with the cooks, and before long he agreed to talk with me about the cafe.

When I encouraged him to talk about himself, he balked; however, one of his cronies yelled out, "Oh, go ahead, Rollie, you old movie star!" His eyes twinkled and he hollered back, "Guess you're right."

With that, he grabbed a cup of coffee and began his tales, and I lost all sense of time. Rollie talked about the two hundred reels of film he had shot of Cuero and its many events over the years. He talked about the extensive collection of photographs he had taken documenting Cuero's

Doll House Cafe

history. He talked about the cassette recordings he had made of Cuero citizens as they shared memories of their lifetime. And all of this since the 1940s.

He told me about the old jukeboxes he had restored over the years. He told me about the custom cars he had built during the 1950s. And then he casually told me about the two years he had served fighting for the United States during World War II. Following that last piece of information, he looked around the room and muttered, "Enough about me. What else did you want to know?"

I asked about the history of the Doll House and learned that in 1935, when the cafe was known as the Old Spanish Garden, Rollie purchased the business for $25. However, at closing, the record of his payment had been lost so he had to cough up another $25. "Not bad for an eighteen-year-old kid right out of high school, wouldn't you say?"

Wanting to rename the business, Rollie did what he does best. He involved Cuero citizens by holding a contest for a new restaurant name. And as irony would have it, the honor went to the Doll House Cafe. He grinned sheepishly, shrugged his broad shoulders, and said, "Guess fair is fair."

In 1948 he installed air conditioning, which put an end to the outdoor beer garden that had been at the cafe when he bought it. In its place Rollie built a miniature golf course for the kids; unfortunately, it went the way of the beer garden. In 1950 he doubled the diner's size and modernized it later that decade.

He paused, then spoke softly of his wife of fifty-six years who died in 1995. After her death he figured it was time to retire, so he sold the business to a local restaurateur, Jerry Rossett, who has since passed away. Jerald, Mr. Rossett's son, took over the diner after Jerry's death.

Knowing a good thing when they saw it, both Rossett men extended an invitation for Rollie to keep coming in and working as long as he wanted. Rollie accepted that invite with open arms, as evidenced by his presence in the cafe at this time.

Looking at his watch, Rollie remarked that it was time for him to go home and get some rest. But before he left, I commented that obviously the fast-food restaurants hadn't put a dent in the Doll House's business. He grinned and declared, "We always had fast food, we just took a little longer."

Doll House Cafe
206 E. Broadway
Cuero, TX 77954
(512) 275-2627

Doll House Cafe

Doll House Cafe

Midway Bar

MIDWAY BAR

We left Cuero and took U.S. 77A to Yorktown. Because it was so late in the afternoon when we entered the city limits, we decided to make a quick run down the main street. We noticed a tavern that had potential, so I jotted its name, the Midway Bar, into my journal for quick reference the next day.

When I stepped through the screen door into the Midway Bar, a translucent amber light enveloped me as I gazed at the tall wooden bar which stretched down the room's left side and the tables that were scattered along the right side.

The narrow room was cool despite not having air conditioning. My eyes moved upward to the bronze-colored tin ceiling then back to the walls. I studied the five landscape murals painted on large canvases that hung high on these walls and carried one's eyes around the room. Their dark tones fused with the room's earthen hues.

As I took a seat at one of the thirteen mismatched barstools, I was intrigued by the room's cotton-like quietness even though two customers at the bar's far end carried on a lively conversation with the man behind the counter. That man looked my way, walked over, and without removing the well-chewed cigar from his mouth, took the order and served the drink.

I looked back toward the bar's floor-to-ceiling store front and realized that the screen mesh stretched across it added to the interior's diaphanous atmosphere. While slowly sipping my beer, I studied the knickknacks behind the bar. Two caught my eye. A coffee cup read, "If you're so smart, why aren't you rich?" And a small sign preached, "If you keep your mouth shut, you won't get in trouble." They lent character to the place.

The bartender returned to his friends, and I watched him manipulate the cigar with his lips as he chattered away. Before long, one of the customers paid his tab and left, and the bartender moved back down the bar to see if I needed another drink. I said no but asked if I could get some historical information about the bar. Introductions were made, and Dalton Borgfeld folded both arms on the counter.

The structure was first built to house a confectionery in the early 1900s. Oscar Jochen then bought out the business in 1935 and converted it into the Midway Bar. Changing hands several times since Mr. Jochen's days, it finally fell to Dalton and Daisy Borgfeld's charge in 1975, who as a pair have continued to keep the place open.

When I asked a few questions about the long-time regulars, he teased, "They're the only things I can't control. Why, a lot of them no longer come in since they're buried in the city cemetery." A boyish grin quickly spread across Dalton's face and he added, "Now actually, most of the customers ARE regulars, it's just that every once in a while a stranger happens by. Like you." I returned his grin.

His voice took on a child-like lilt as he talked about the good old western days

Midway Bar

when people rode their horses right up to the bar. He pointed at the original doors, which were folded back against the side walls, and explained that years ago he had to screen in the front. "Something to do with a health code," he shrugged.

The other customer called out, "See you, Dalton," then waved and left through a back door. As I watched him leave, I noticed a section off to the back where sunshine through an open door spotlighted pearlescent dominoes scattered upon two wooden tables. Dalton noticed my gaze. "A handful of regular domino players still come in, so I always leave the tables set up and the back door open," he clarified.

We then talked about his partner, Daisy, who is known around these parts as the Queen of the Silver Dollar. Together, this duo orchestrates a balancing act to keep the bar open with Dalton working during the day and Daisy during the night. But he said that their hours have dwindled as the number of regular customers has tapered off.

He looked off into space for a second, then proclaimed, "I'm happy being here. Seems like the longer I have the bar, the crazier I get and the more I like it." With that he picked up a stack of Polaroid pictures and leisurely shared them with me, snapshot by snapshot.

Dalton checked his watch and I knew that even though it was only three in the afternoon it must be getting close to break time. We walked to the screen door, and just as we stepped out onto the sidewalk, he said, "See where I'm standing? I can't see a car on either side of the street." I looked up and down and he was right, the street was empty.

As I walked to my car, the large, folding doors creaked closed as Dalton Borgfeld disengaged the world outside on the street from the world inside the Midway Bar.

Midway Bar
633 6th Street
Yorktown, TX 78164
(512) 564-3129

Midway Bar

Gruene Hall

GRUENE HALL

The drive south from Austin along Interstate 35 led us just outside of New Braunfels to a hamlet that serves as a reminder that some of life's greatest gifts can be found in little, out-of-the-way places. It was there that I unwrapped the story behind one of those gifts, Gruene Hall.

After the drive down the main road, I noted the casualness with which people walked in and out of the businesses that lined both sides. The storefronts were pictures of charm and antiquity. At the end of the short street, I found myself facing a building nestled between a grist mill restaurant and a bed and breakfast inn. There in the middle of those two sites stood the ever popular Texas dance spot Gruene Hall.

Its whitewashed facade held no fancy airs. Once I stepped through the double screen doors, it was as if I had entered into a world without worry. Every table in the front room was occupied with small social coteries, the members of which didn't appear in too big a hurry.

There were no barstools at the counter yet three people stood before it and drank cold beers, so I took a spot alongside them and turned in my order. Scanning the walls, I noticed cowboy hats, antlers, and photos, and on closer observation I realized that one man kept cropping up in many of the pictures.

Curious about this repeated image, I asked the bartender about the man in the photos, and although the young bartender did not know the man's name, he confirmed that the old-time resident had been a long-running regular at the hall. The bartender stood with the drink in one hand and pointed back to the wall with his other hand. "See those hats," he said, "They're all his."

He then set the drink down on the counter. When I tilted my head back to take the first long quaff, I found myself peering past the bartender, through an open window, and directly into an enormous dance hall.

Without hesitation I rounded the corner and headed into this cavernous room outfitted with well-worn plank flooring that had old license plates randomly embedded in it. Except for a dance floor and stage at the room's far end, long picnic tables filled most of the area. People sat either on the tables' benches or literally on top of the tables themselves.

Although no music played at the moment, several children whirled and twirled until they fell giggling onto the wooden dance floor. A mother and her young daughter swayed to and fro to music playing in their heads. And all around people jabbered away and completely disregarded the sultry summer heat that seeped in through open windows. No one made the slightest effort to leave.

I crossed the dance floor, walked past some teenagers shooting pool, and went out the side door to the old beer garden.

Gruene Hall

Several people sat at tables under a dense canopy of shade trees. Children ran about playing a game of kick the can. A couple of elderly men tossed horseshoes. A group of motorcyclists gathered over near the front fence. And a family of five sat on a blanket and ate their lunch.

After a walk around the yard, I returned to the dance hall to learn about Gruene's background. This German settlement, which dated back to the 1800s, had its roots in cotton farming. In 1878 Henry Gruene built the original dance hall and saloon on this site for his surrounding tenant farmers. Since Mr. Gruene's days, ownership has changed hands several times. The business belonged to Kurt Schaefer from 1960 until 1974 before he sold it to Mary Jane Nalley and Pat Molak, who reopened the legendary hall in the winter of 1975.

One of their first goals was to bring back the sounds of live music to these historic walls, and bring it back they have. The list of great musicians, both local and out-of-state, who have made Gruene Hall an arena for their talents is endless.

There have been no major changes to the building's structure, and even the original bar still stands, although it has been enlarged in stages over the years. In order to maintain the hall's authenticity, Mary Jane and Pat have no plans to alter it, not even by adding air conditioning.

Gruene Hall, also known for its family orientation, bills Sundays from midafternoon until around nine at night specifically as family time, and at almost any of those Sunday gigs you will find just as many children on the dance floor as adults.

Mary Jane Nalley offered a final statement that captured the true essence of this historical landmark when she expressed that "dancing knows no size, no age, no color, and there is some sort of spirit at Gruene Hall that just makes it a good-feeling place."

Gruene Hall
1601 Hunter Road
New Braunfels, TX 78130
(830) 629-5077

Gruene Hall

Gruene Hall

Patt's Drug Store

PATT'S DRUG STORE

After an overnight stay in Gruene, we left the tiny town around 10 A.M. and headed south on Interstate 35. Energized by the prospect of a future find, we hit the San Antonio city limits with high hopes. We maneuvered into the heart of the Alamo city, passing lush landscapes and stucco structures before espying the storefront that announced the arrival at Patt's Drug Store on Broadway.

Entering its corner door, I was disappointed as the building seemed to house only a modern drugstore. I had been hoping for that holy grail—the sacred soda fountain—but there was no sign of one. I focused my attention on the pharmacist working quietly behind his counter and the customers browsing the aisles. Then the unmistakable aroma of grilled hamburgers and onions drifted over.

Although the view was obscured by the labyrinthine shelf units, I guessed that the fountain lay beyond those walls of merchandise. Traipsing through the maze, I found my instincts to be correct. There it stood, a beautiful soda fountain whose original flair had been preserved.

Its gray-and-white, L-shaped Formica counter cupped the right end of the fountain area. Its nine royal blue barstools stood out against the counter's red base and the black-and-white tiled floor. Three large booths, which were butted up against the left end of this counter, ran along the fountain's length.

I sat at the counter's curved end in order to observe the fountain, the cook, and the eleven diners. Some customers lingered over their meals while others ate quickly. Still others scurried in, picked up orders, chatted with the cook, and rushed back to work.

The cook and waitress, who made constant eye-to-eye contact with the customers, forged a sense of comfort. With that encouraged ease, I began a conversation with the cook, who immediately spoke of the long-standing popularity of the fountain and grill, and he recognized the customers who have made Patt's a regular stop. Then he boasted that the drugstore served some of the best home-cooked meals a person could find in town. Since it was noon, I decided to challenge that boast by ordering the daily hamburger special. I sat back to wait patiently.

During the wait I approached Greg Raley, the pharmacist, to try to get some information about the drugstore's history. He first explained that he has served as both manager and pharmacist for many years. Then he explained that his stepfather, John Mohrmann, has owned the business since 1985. However, he suggested I call Jo Stewart, whose father originally owned the center in which the drugstore sits, in order to learn more history.

I wrote down her telephone number, checked on the food, and seeing that it was not yet ready strode over to the wooden phone booth at the fountain's end. As I stepped inside and closed the bifold door,

Patt's Drug Store

I felt encapsulated in a soundproof box. Through its windows I watched the fountain's life play out mutely before me, then I dropped the money into the pay phone's coin slots and waited to connect with Ms. Stewart. Fortunately, it didn't require much goading to talk her into taking time from her schedule to talk about the drugstore's history.

Her father, Colonel Benjamin F. Chadwick, built Chadwick Center around 1940. (The old Chadwick Center is now known as Stewart Center.) At that time the original drugstore was constructed with its corner door opening onto a patio that faced up the hill where the Seven Oaks Country Club stood. Around 1945 the country club moved and the patio was enclosed. Homer "Patt" Patterson later bought the building, renamed it Patt's Drug Store, and ran the establishment until 1985 when he sold it to Mr. Mohrmann.

When I asked about the store's authenticity, Ms. Stewart said that although the pharmacy has been remodeled several times, the fountain area remains relatively as it was in the 1940s. That explained the bold colors, the old telephone booth, the tiled floor, and the spirit of the place.

After the interview I slid open the door, stepped back into the store, and noted that the food had arrived. I took a seat so I could put the cook's bravado to the test. The hamburger was juicy. The french fries were crispy. And the shake was silky. No doubt about it, he had secured his right to sing the praises about the good food at Patt's. And so with a palate that was pleased as punch, I conceded the stop had been a fruitful one.

Later in a phone conversation with Mr. Raley I learned that the fountain is temporarily closed, but there are plans to reopen it. This information nudged a heavy-hearted question that had accompanied many of my Texas travels. How long will we be able to enjoy these legendary spots before they disappear from the pages of our living history?

Patt's Drug Store
5150 Broadway
San Antonio, TX 78209
(210) 826-0616

Patt's Drug Store

Olmos Pharmacy

OLMOS PHARMACY

After spending some time at the drugstore on Broadway in San Antonio, we followed the advice of a fellow diner and made our way back through the city streets toward Hildebrand. It was there that we noticed the small corner building with the 1930s storefront. Bold letters encircled a clock above the front door and announced Olmos Pharmacy.

Inside the store, the soda fountain counter and booths sparked with activity. Only three of the fifteen army green swivel barstools at the tan counter were available, and none of the five booths were open. I claimed one of the vacated stools, sat down, and quickly eyed the counter's worn spots that indicated years of elbows and hot plates. Glancing beyond the counter, I peered through an elliptical window, which not only provided a view of people and cars passing by but also served as a point for sunlight to enter and glisten off the back counter's polished chrome.

"What can I get you?" asked a soft voice. I turned and there stood Rachel, a tiny woman with salt-and-pepper hair. Since their milkshakes had been highly recommended, I ordered one. When she finally placed the glass and chrome shaker on the counter, I asked if she had worked at Olmos for long.

"Long? Well, let's see. I've worked here for as long as I can remember," she replied in a matter-of-fact tone. At the first opportunity, I asked if she had been making shakes for that long period of time, and she chuckled. "Yep. I've been making shakes for thirty-three years." I raised my eyebrows in acknowledgment. She turned to leave but then sashayed back around and added, "You think that's a long time to work here; well, Sam's been the delivery boy here for over forty years."

Later, she added that she has seen generation after generation make Olmos a regular stop, and that she has seen all these regulars "grow up, go off and get on with their lives, and then come back with their own kids."

It was at that point that an older lady who sat two stools down from me leaned over. She mentioned she had overheard our conversation while drinking her coffee and just couldn't resist joining in. She talked about how she had been coming to the pharmacy since her youth to enjoy its food and friendly atmosphere. "It is simply part of the pleasure of my life," she added softly.

As she left, a lady who sat with her daughter in a booth behind me spoke up. She, too, had overheard our conversations and knew of a few places with counters that might be added to the list. And then as if it had become a community effort, a man and his wife who also sat at the counter said they knew of a couple of places, too. They scooched over.

Shortly, I had the map spread out on the counter and we were all busy swapping tales and marking towns to visit. This lively

exchange lasted for ten or fifteen minutes, and none of the fountain workers rushed us. As a matter of fact, the opened map was an invitation for the workers to join in. Rachel continued to make shakes as customers came and went.

After plotting future excursions, I then asked Rachel for some historical information on Olmos, but she said, "Oh, you'll need to talk with Mr. Stone, but he only works on Thursday and Friday."

Weeks later, I called George Stone and explained the project. He gladly talked about Mr. L. D. Gilmore, who opened Gilmore's Pharmacy on this spot in 1938. Mr. Gilmore ran the business until 1952 when he sold it to Mr. Richard Sandidge, who then changed the name to Olmos Pharmacy. Mr. Sandidge was owner until 1970. That was when George Stone bought the drugstore and began his role as owner and main pharmacist for twenty-four years. In 1994 he sold the business to John Dodd, who is now both full-time pharmacist and business owner. Mr. Stone explained that he has retained ownership of the building and still works in the pharmacy part-time.

Then in a wistful voice George Stone added, "You know, I used to come in to this drugstore when I was a kid. Why, I used to play little league baseball near here for the Olmos Pharmacy Little League team. I just never dreamed I'd have any connection with the pharmacy at that time."

There was a moment of quiet, then he turned the table on the interview. He asked if I had noticed anything odd about the letters spelling out "Olmos" on the outside clock. I thought a second, said no, and he quipped, "Well, next time you're in, look closely at that clock."

Olmos Pharmacy
3902 McCullough
San Antonio, TX 78212
(210) 822-3361

Olmos Pharmacy

Arkey Blue's Silver Dollar

ARKEY BLUE'S SILVER DOLLAR

From San Antonio we headed northwest on State Highway 16. As we drove along, the surrounding vistas took on new features. Rolling hills expanded in peaceful swells. And the hue of the open skies deepened to cornflower blue. After about forty-five minutes we pulled into Bandera, a true Texas-style mecca with a western flair. Main Street offered Busbee's BBQ, Bank's Steakhouse, the Old Spanish Trail Restaurant, the Western Ivy Ice Cream Shop, and of course, Arkey Blue's Silver Dollar, a honky-tonk that touted live western music.

I pulled open the heavy wooden door only to find myself peering down a staircase that stretched into the cellar-like depths of a darkened room. After taking a moment to adjust my eyes to the dimness, I studied the multitude of photos, calendars, and framed articles that lined the wall. Pausing periodically to observe these items, I at last reached the last step and found a medium-sized dance floor at the base of the stairway that offered a sprinkling of sawdust for some slick boot-scooting and band equipment that rested like electronic scarecrows waiting to be brought to life.

Everywhere I looked, the room boiled over with memorabilia—photos and articles of Arkey Blue and his band, pictures of Hank Williams, Elvis, and local patrons—and all were frozen moments that documented life at the Silver Dollar. The antique jukebox, velvet paintings, and old guitars amplified the saloon's atmosphere.

I imagined that the large stone fireplace, which stood cold and lifeless on the summer day I visited, would blaze with life throughout the winter to create a warm and snug retreat where the guests and musicians could kick back in their chairs and kick up their boots.

Three young men joked with one another as they shot pool in an area skirted by tables and booths. Another guy busied himself by trying to beat the odds at the Dolly Parton pinball machine. A group of men and women sitting at one of the long tables appeared relaxed and laid back as they sipped their drinks.

As I made my way past these small groups of contented customers, a drawn-out wail of a whippoorwill train whistle resounded in the room. The pool players laughed, the patrons laughed, and I laughed. Then one of the guys yelled over to me, "Welcome to Arkey's. You've just been blessed by our very own Choo-Choo Perkins." Choo-Choo flashed his rascally grin my way then turned back to the mid-afternoon visit with his pals. (Mr. Perkins has since passed away.)

I found a seat at the small bar and took note of the natural light that streamed into the dusky room from an open side door. The light cast a silvery-blue tint onto the bar's varnished countertop and illuminated the names and dates trenched into its

Arkey Blue's Silver Dollar

wooden planks. I asked around and soon discovered that no one knew the counter's exact age, but everyone present agreed it was the same one that was there when Ralph Mitchell was the owner.

Mr. Mitchell purchased the building and opened up the Foxhole at the beginning of the 1950s. He ran a prosperous business for many years before he passed the torch on to a Fredericksburg native Arkey Juenke. Arkey Blue (as Mr. Juenke is known) bought the business on May 5, 1968, and immediately doubled the space to mark the beginning of his rich, successful legacy.

For over thirty years Arkey has followed his dream. He has built a special place where people of all ages and all backgrounds gather for good cheer and good company. He has built a haven where musicians regularly stop by to sing and pick tunes. And he has built a studio where he can play and record his own music, often sharing the stage with local country music legends who make the Silver Dollar a part of their venue.

In his lifetime, Arkey Blue has not only given chase to his dream but has also caught it, ensuring that anyone who walks down that steep staircase into the Silver Dollar will feel welcomed in his underground castle.

Arkey Blue's Silver Dollar
308 Main Street
Bandera, TX 78003
(830) 796-8826

Arkey Blue's Silver Dollar

Arkey Blue's Silver Dollar

Sisterdale General Store

SISTERDALE GENERAL STORE

The next day around 10 A.M. we headed due east to Interstate 10. From there, we turned onto FM 473 and passed pasture after pasture polka-dotted with woolly sheep. At a spot so small you'd miss it if you blinked your eyes sat Sisterdale, a tiny village cradled in a dale between East Sister Creek and West Sister Creek. The town's solitary street was still, yet the few cars parked in front of one of the three buildings signaled a smidgen of activity. We pulled in next to a pickup truck, and that's when we noticed the sign, Sisterdale General Store.

A window framed by red-and-white gingham cafe curtains granted a peek inside at a counter of medium length. When I pushed open the front door the unmistakable click-clacking of dominoes braked to a stop, and simultaneously a roomful of eyes looked up. However, within a matter of seconds the four men had resumed their domino game, and a lady rose from the back table where she sat with four other women. She walked behind the bar and waited.

I took a seat at one of the six modern stools that stood before the exquisite antique counter. The lady filled my order then returned to the group of women. I closed my eyes and listened as the women's spirited voices harmonized with the men's steady drones, creating a synchronized symphony of high and low tones.

Accompanied by their magpie music, I examined the back bar. Its richly toned wood was enhanced by intricate designs. Two mounted deer heads on either side of this wooden piece of art created a balance of that which is man-made and that which is not. Looking closely, I found much could be seen in the reflection of the back bar's mirror. On the opposite wall a hand-painted mural illustrated Sisterdale's history. Next to it a shuffleboard stretched toward the back of the room, and above the game board a stuffed deer head served as a hat rack for six caps. I slyly looked askance to watch the intense faces and strong hands of the men playing dominoes.

An old rotary phone rang, and the lady who had filled my order rose to answer it. As she talked, she ran her hand along the top of the one-hundred-year-old cooler butted up to the counter's end. Somehow both the phone and the refrigerator fit the room's modest, utilitarian decor.

While she chatted on the phone, I walked past her into the adjacent room where I discovered a large area that housed a meeting space and a grocery store. Pastoral murals painted on the back wall set the formal tone for a raised platform, a piano, bookcases, and dining tables. I surveyed the room's front portion, which served as a small grocery store, but what caught my eye was the checkout counter whose worn Formica hinted at years of use.

When I walked back into the other room, I explained the project to the

Sisterdale General Store

gracious lady who introduced herself as Valerija Woolvin. Valerija then settled against the back bar and began recalling the general store's history as she had heard it. Mr. and Mrs. Harry Hill built the store in 1954, the same year that the old saloon and dance hall which stood across the street closed. And as if by chance, it was that closing which ensured that the saloon's one-hundred-year-old ornate curly pine counter and back bar would become a cherished addition to the new general store. Seventeen years later, in 1971, Valerija moved to Sisterdale from Mississippi, and in 1978 she assumed control of the business.

Before she could get out another word, the ladies' booming laughter served as bait to lure Valerija and me over to their table. We took the bait, and for nearly an hour it felt like a family reunion where familiar tales were shared.

In between stories, talk turned to one of the women, Leatrice Ransleben, who was born in 1930 in the white house across the street from the general store. They reminisced about the time she was crowned "Queen of Sisterdale" at the 1947 centennial celebration.

Then one of the ladies looked my way and added, "Yeah, can you imagine. The queen of Sisterdale used to drive her two dogs and a buck deer around in her convertible." The laughter echoed off the walls. Noting my puzzled look, Leatrice quickly explained that her dad had found a deer near death and brought it home. She had fed the sickly creature with a bottle to nurse him back to good health and soon found she had a friend for life.

Amid the softening chuckles of this close-knit group, I checked my watch and noted it was time to head out. As I walked toward the door, one man extended an open invitation to come back any Tuesday or Thursday for a game of dominoes. As simple as that, I had been welcomed into their circle of esprit de corps.

Sisterdale General Store
1215 Sisterdale Road
Boerne, TX 78006
(210) 324-6767

Sisterdale General Store

Sisterdale General Store

INGENHUETT STORE

The next stop was just a stone's throw away from Sisterdale. We followed FM 473 west, crossed Interstate 10, and hooked up with State Highway 27, and where those two paths intersect we found the small town of Comfort.

We parked the car on High Street and rambled alongside beautiful limestone structures that lined the streets and dated back to the late nineteenth century. Every surrounding building highlighted the town's heritage. Blocks into the stroll, we spied a porch sign that read: Peter Ingenhuett, Fancy Groceries, Hardware and Implements.

Four concrete steps led up to open screen doors where a customer waved goodbye to the man with blond hair who stood behind the checkout counter. I passed the departing customer and walked in just as this tow-headed man turned to help an elderly gentleman find a rubber tip for his cane.

Once indoors I found people traversing the aisles between shelves whose low heights enhanced the room's openness. I strolled to the back of the room to check out the large meat and dairy refrigerators. While some customers actually shopped for groceries, I noted most simply enjoyed an awe-struck exploration through a place seemingly devoid of modern amenities.

When I returned to the store's front area, the man behind the counter introduced himself, and after hearing what I was looking for, Greg Krauter said, "You've come to the right place." In one fluid movement, he rested his foot on the lower end of the checkout counter and his elbow upon one knee. He bent forward and casually began sharing his family's business history.

His great-great grandfather, Peter J. Ingenhuett, originally built his mercantile business in 1867 on the site where the old Ingenhuett-Faust Hotel stands. Then in 1880 he hired a San Antonio architect, Alfred Giles, to design and build this building. In 1891 Peter's son, Paul, assumed ownership and the business grew to a multifaceted complex which included a private bank, a hotel, a post office, a saloon, an opera house, a livery stable, and a cotton yard. After thirty years, Paul handed the business over to his son, Peter C. Ingenhuett, who further expanded it to include the merchandising of farm equipment and implements.

By the mid-1930s the establishment competed nationally in a mohair and wool partnership, which was headquartered at this site, and then in 1955 the business went to Paul's daughter, Gladys Krauter. Greg proudly added that Gladys, his mother, was an independent woman who ran the business along with his father, Jimmy, until her death in March of 1995. At that time Greg, a fifth generation Ingenhuett, stepped in to help his dad keep the family legacy alive.

Ingenhuett Store

Assuming the role of tour guide, Greg then led me through a connecting doorway into another expansive room. He pointed out the old bolt case dating back to the 1880s and the old sliding ladder still used to collect items from the bins that reached up to the eighteen-foot ceiling. He proudly showed off a unique rifle shot case built in 1879.

Next he showed me the counters. First, there was the old bank counter built in 1869 and remodeled in 1948. It still sits in front of the 1891 walk-in vault and the 1948 freestanding vault. Following that one, there was the counter specifically built in 1948 to display nails. And last but not least, there was another counter—also built in 1948—over which years and years of farm implement transactions were made.

Greg and I then returned to the grocery store. I drank a soda while Greg waited on customers, wrote tickets by hand, and rang up the sales on the family's old hand-cranked calculator.

As I sipped on my soft drink, in walked Corwin Carlisle Connell, a polished gentleman with angel-white hair. Corwin grinned, greeted Greg, then pulled a soda from out of the cooler and hopped atop the antique machine.

Greg told Corwin about the book project, and as if on cue, Corwin began talking about the years between 1938 and 1941 when his father, a former Methodist minister, had moved the family to Comfort. He nostalgically remembered buying BBs from Mr. Ingenhuett for 5¢ and then riding his bike down to the Guadalupe River to shoot his BB gun.

However, his fondest memory was of Gladys Krauter. Almost as if he was seeing her again, Corwin recalled the adventurous Ingenhuett daughter as she buzzed the town with her Piper J-5 Cruiser and became Corwin's first real-life hero.

The storytelling ceased shortly before the sun slipped over the horizon. I watched out the screen door as dusk began to settle about the town, then I bid a gracious goodbye. I placed the empty pop bottle in the rack, walked out through the double doors, and strolled into the softening twilight that was descending upon historical High Street.

Peter J. Ingenhuett Store
830-834 High Street
Comfort, TX 78013
(830) 995-2149

Ingenhuett Store

Ingenhuett Store

Kitty's Place

KITTY'S PLACE

After reading an article in a local Comfort newspaper about a favorite watering hole for Ingram locals, we knew where to head for the next leg of the expedition.

The following morning we had trouble locating the Ingram watering hole, but then the gods on Mount Olympus swirled the waters of destiny and guided us to a sprite of a man walking up the road. We pulled over to ask for directions to Kitty's Place, and with cowboy hat in hand, this pint-sized local quipped, "If you'll give me a ride to Rosa's, I'll show you where it is." I flung open the back door and in he hopped.

Before long, Jessie Lee was providing directions to Kitty's Place as he chattered on about being the "honorary mayor of Ingram," about the good life in Ingram, and about the good food at Rosa's. Once at the restaurant, Jessie hopped out, tipped his hat, and hollered, "Thanks for the ride. Nice to meet you."

The short trek back to the local hangout on Old Ingram Loop 27 didn't take long. Once there, I recorded a few notes about how life on the street appeared sluggish and how the air seemed to resonate with tiny violins being tuned by summer crickets. Then I noted the giant tree with branches that sprawled open like an umbrella to protect the small red building which housed Kitty's Place.

The screen door slapped behind me as I entered, and the two gentlemen customers looked up, but in nothing flat they resumed their private discourse. A petite woman at the back of the room stood and waited while I selected a seat at the counter. After she filled my drink order, she excused herself and returned to finish her lunch.

A short while later, one of the men walked to the old cooler, pulled out another drink, put some money on the counter, and sat back down. We all drank in silence and I studied the stacks of papers, pharmaceutical items, signs, and pictures that filled the shelves behind the counter.

Finished with her meal, the woman moved over behind the counter. I made my introduction and soon became privy to the stories behind Kitty's Place, told to me by Miss Kitty West Pumphrey herself.

First, she recounted how her former father-in-law, J. J. Maxwell, had built Maxwell Drugstore in the early 1920s. At that time he put in the marble-topped soda fountain and the old back bar that stand in the store to this day. She pointed to the old hand-cranked cash register that was J. J.'s and said, "I still use it because I believe in the old saying, 'If it ain't broke, don't fix it.'" Then she smiled and added that although the old soda dispensers don't work, she doesn't have any plans to get rid of them because they are gentle reminders of the early days.

Kitty's Place

A man entered through the back door at that point, got a drink out of the refrigerator, and sat down at the counter. This regular customer for over forty-one years listened as Kitty talked about the 1930s when J. J. moved his business closer to the new highway and sold this store to his son, James Maxwell. James, just like his father, was a pharmacist.

Kitty recalled that shortly after James bought the place, he proposed marriage to her, she accepted, they were married, and they began a joint venture in life and business. Once James had secured a beer license he built the second counter, which still butts up against the old soda fountain.

She briefly talked about her husband's death over thirty years ago, mentioning that after he passed away she decided to hang onto the business and rename it Kitty's Place. I smiled at this fitting name. When you look around, you see feline items everywhere. There are cat ceramics, cat pictures, cat signs, and cat T-shirts, not to mention Candy, the long-haired black-and-white house cat who has the run of the place.

Out of curiosity, I asked Miss Kitty about the twenty or so mismatched chairs lined up against the far wall. A slight grin danced across her face as she glanced at the other customers and teased, "All the regular's got their own chair, so you have to be careful not to sit in one of them." They nodded and grinned.

Upon conclusion of this relaxed and peaceful visit, I couldn't help but feel that Miss Kitty is indeed a woman of Southern charm and Kitty's Place is definitely a spot for Southern comfort.

Kitty's Place
208 Old Ingram Loop
Ingram, TX 78025
(830) 367-5783

Kitty's Place

Pampell's Antiques & Soda Fountain

PAMPELL'S ANTIQUES & SODA FOUNTAIN

Leaving Ingram, we hopscotched over to Kerrville after learning about a soda fountain the town was rumored to have. We arrived around 3 o'clock in the afternoon and drove about. Soon, we found Pampell's Antiques & Soda Fountain—an elegant, two-story building—on the corner of Water Street and Highway 16. We parked, peeked in, and spotted the counter.

As I entered, I felt like a character in a classic novel where boy meets girl at the local soda fountain. Yesterday's treasures filled the downstair and balcony areas. Kids and adults sat at the old-fashioned turn-of-the-century counter and savored midday snacks. I joined them and ordered a shake and a sandwich.

The polished chrome back counter ran the length of the building; its stainless steel refrigerators and syrup dispensers glistened. An old Hamilton blender was surrounded by tin milkshake holders and banana split dishes. Old soda dispensers looked like shiny, poised horse heads while thirteen pedestal barstools stood like soldiers at attention. The scene evoked a sense of regality.

Pampell's counter design reminded me of the one at Olmos Pharmacy in San Antonio since both faced large plate-glass windows, portals through which diners could daydream as they watched people and cars zip back and forth. Through this portal, tendrils of sunlight caressed the room with a silken glow.

I twirled around on the barstool, placed both elbows on the counter, and craned my neck upward to study the balcony that brimmed with antiques; it wrapped around two-thirds of the second floor. The store's high ceiling displayed large, ornately stenciled walnut beams.

The waitress tapped my shoulder, and I turned around to find my food waiting for me. The customers' voices mixed with the whirring blender, the ringing phone, and the never ending swishing and swooshing of the front door as it opened and closed. I ate slowly, enjoying the moment.

As the waitress gathered my empty plate and glass, I asked questions about the history of the building and she answered the ones she could. Then, she introduced me to Doris and Mary Jo, who eagerly began to relate their stories.

They explained how John L. Pampell had purchased the building in 1901 when it was known as the M. V. Gregory Hotel. He converted the first floor into a drugstore and grocery store, the second floor's front section into a 450-seat opera and play house, and the second floor's back section into a confectionery for the manufacturing and sale of candy and his own strawberry cream soda.

We walked toward the back of the room, and Mary Jo pointed out the stylish

Pampell's Antiques & Soda Fountain

bar placed against the wall. She explained that Mr. Pampell—known as Mr. Johnny to his friends and customers—had attended the 1904 St. Louis World's Fair and purchased this piece and the existing soda fountain. "Just imagine," she whispered, "they've been here for over ninety years."

As I followed the two women into the basement, they talked about the cola franchise Milton, Mr. Pampell's son, had bought in 1916. They spoke about the many successful years of cranking out sodas with the biggest year being 1948, when the Pampell men turned out about 1,500 bottles an hour.

Then the two women talked about the inevitable changes. In 1927 Milton removed part of the upstairs flooring and built the existing balcony. He bricked the exterior, moved the old back bar, and installed the large windows that face State Highway 16.

They recalled the heyday of curb service during the 1940s and 1950s. They laughed about Mr. Johnny's refusal to put in air conditioning, and how it was only after his death in 1958 that Milton was able to do so.

They agreed that even though there have been a lot of changes, John and Milton Pampell's passionate spirit lives on through the efforts of current owners, Jon and Sandy Wolfmuller. (The Wolfmullers arc in the process of selling the fountain in order to dedicate time to their bookstore on Water Street.)

When I spoke with the Wolfmullers, they explained that when they bought the building in 1989 everything except the original back bar and soda fountain had been auctioned off and the place had been closed up for about two and one-half years.

Together—with a lot of love and hard work—they have restored much to its original state, breathing life back into this legendary place. Their commitment to maintaining the fountain's authenticity was summed up when Jon said, "I believe the place offers nostalgia, and whoever owns it has to keep it that way because people bring their kids into Pampell's to experience an old-time soda fountain and jukebox."

As I gathered my things to leave, eighty-nine-year-old Jimmie Stone shared that he had been a soda jerk for Mr. Pampell. Then he left me with these parting words: "This is a wonderful place where the little ones can enjoy coming in to get a bowl of ice cream." I smiled and thought to myself, I guess there is a "little one" in all of us.

Pampell's Antiques & Soda Fountain
701 Water Street
Kerrville, TX 78028
(830) 257-8484

Pampell's Antiques & Soda Fountain

Lock Drugs

LOCK DRUGS

Using Austin as a home base for some short day trips meant being able to spend more time to search for little close-in treasure troves. Such was the case when we drove east on State Highway 71 and spotted another of the Texas "historical district" signs sprinkled throughout the state. Following its lead, we turned onto Loop 150 and headed into Bastrop. I felt anticipation grip my spirit.

Loop 150 travels alongside an old trestle bridge that spans the Colorado River and leads into the downtown area. Within minutes we had passed the Bastrop County courthouse, the old county jail, and the local historical museum. After turning onto Main Street, I noted the single blinking red light that winked like a beacon at the crossroads; it hinted of townspeople who are not in too big a rush as they go about their day.

However, in contrast to this subliminal message, which signaled a domain of dalliance, Bastrop's downtown buzzed with activity. A majority of the old buildings were occupied, and their doors constantly opened and closed to reveal flurries of busyness. Every single parking spot along the main drag was filled so the only option was to park on a side street.

The maneuverings down the main street sidewalk led me through clusters of people before I found the Chamber of Commerce. As soon as its door swished shut the woman at the front desk cheerfully greeted me and, as if accustomed to visitors' questions about the location of a rumored, old-time soda fountain, lit into a brief narrative of the place. Then rising from her desk, she walked to the door, stepped out onto the sidewalk, and gave me

directions to this local landmark. It didn't take long for me to march right over and check it out.

The drugstore's freshly painted white exterior was bejeweled by forest green and burgundy trim. Its storefront displayed the building's historical marker, and its windows featured arrangements of old medicine bottles and drugstore memorabilia.

Inside, two old ceiling fans dangled from a twenty-foot-high ceiling that was encircled by ornate molding accented with gold leaf applications. The fans swirled slowly above five soda shop tables. At one of those tables, four adults drank coffee and chattered, while at another a mother and her son enjoyed soft drinks. To my left four kids occupied barstools at the marble counter, their happy faces reflected in the back bar's mirror. The customers represented an assembly of all ages.

A furled American flag stood in one corner. Music played from a portable radio sitting atop the shelf unit that consisted of old wooden apothecary drawers. A Hamilton blender whirred in the background.

I ordered a shake and sat down at one of the tables. Half of the customers appeared to be locals while the other half looked much like me, a tourist just paying a call. Inevitably, as older visitors stepped into the

Lock Drugs

store and discovered the soda fountain, a smile would travel across their faces as though they were flipping through their pages of memories. And it seemed that no matter who entered, they lingered for a while.

When things slowed down a bit, I asked about the drugstore's history, and that's when one of the women behind the pharmacy's counter filled me in on the legacy. Dating back to the 1850s, the business began as a carpenter shop owned by Mr. Reynolds and Mr. Gillespie. Up until 1905 it ran the gamut from storehouse to saloon and finally to a drugstore run by W. J. Wiley. Wiley's Drugstore continued under W. J.'s direction until April of 1967, when it became Belle's Emporium after being purchased by Mr. and Mrs. Oren Eskew. Three years later David Lock, the current pharmacist and a former Bastrop mayor, bought the business and renamed it Lock Drugs. He later sold the property and business to John Mohrmann in 1979. (Mr. Mohrmann also owns a San Antonio drugstore.)

After learning about its more than 140-year-old history, the building and soda fountain took on an even more hallowed spirit. I closed my eyes and pictured a quaint turn-of-the-century scene. In it women in their long, full dresses stood before the marble counter. Men in their top hats stopped by for an afternoon break from a long day's work. And children with their freckled faces stared goggled-eyed at the soda jerk as he piled scoop upon scoop of ice cream into a dish. Then I looked around more closely at the customers sitting presently at the counter and tables and realized how some things remain constant.

That's when an image tickled my thoughts. I pictured Norman Rockwell sitting astride his stool, easel and paints set up before him. There he was, pipe in mouth, hunkered forward as he scrutinized this modern-day setting before immortalizing yet another idyllic American scene.

Lock Drugs
1003 Main Street
Bastrop, TX 78602
(512) 321-2422

Citizens Pharmacy

CITIZENS PHARMACY

After leaving Bastrop yesterday, a return to Austin for the night was a must before heading out once again. The eastwardly search continued along State Highway 290 in hopes that the day's random journeys would be as successful as the previous one. We drove; we searched; we drove some more, but it seemed that the discovery of a new prospect mocked us. That is until we arrived in Brenham.

After a relaxed sojourn through Brenham's city streets and surrounding countryside, we understood why people flock to this area in springtime. You have the best of two worlds: One offers streets of antiquity, while the other offers fields of bluebonnets. And on the corner of Main and Baylor in downtown Brenham sits Citizens Pharmacy, a pot of gold that marks the junction of these two worlds.

Entering the pharmacy's corner door, I came face-to-face with a horseshoe-shaped counter that corralled a long soda fountain. Business was thriving. Seven people sat at the counter, and fourteen people occupied six booths. Without hesitation, I selected one of the turquoise vinyl stools on the counter's far side.

Time-worn spots speckled the white-and-beige Formica top, and the foot ledge that ran along the entire counter also showed signs of heavy use. The overall place reflected a 1950s decor.

A sprightly woman, who had worked at the pharmacy for twenty-five years, seemingly skated over and took my order before introducing me to Bubba Kolbe, the man who had worked at the pharmacy for thirty-two years and who now served as the manager. Almost at once he explained that the previous owner, Bubba Lehrmann Jr. (a good friend of Mr. Kolbe's), had owned the store for over forty years before his death in September of 1995.

Mr. Kolbe talked about the pharmacy's history as if it was something he did every-day. He explained that although much has remained the same since it was built in the late 1800s, it has changed hands several times and received a face-lift every once in a while. And one of those face-lifts involved modernizing the soda fountain and counter during the 1950s. He boasted about the employees, fountain, and counter who bring life to the pharmacy, and how the fusion of these three elements provides a neighborly, social gathering spot for both Brenham citizens and out-of-town guests.

While we talked, a few people came and left, but most came and stayed. There was barely an idle moment during it all. When asked if this was typical activity, Bubba replied, "Oh my, yes! And it gets even more crowded around 9 o'clock in the morning and 3 o'clock in the afternoon when the coffee drinkers gather to catch up on the latest news."

1¢
WEIGHT
———
HOROSCOPE
AND
WEIGHT
5¢

AMERICAN
SCALE
MFG. CO.
WASHINGTON
D.C.

Just then, Patsy Johnson came over to ask Bubba about a customer's prescription. Before she returned to work, I learned she has worked at Citizens for over twenty years and has been a pharmacist since 1947.

During the brief conversation with Patsy, Bubba had left for a moment and had returned carrying an object as if it were sacred. Carefully, he flipped through the yellowed sheets of the old remedy book and stopped at various pages to point out the handwritten notes placed in the margins by Fred Heineke, one of the previous owners of Citizens Pharmacy. As I checked out the many scribbled notations scattered throughout this small volume, certain remedies that ran the gamut from ringworm treatments to cancer pastes to hair tonics piqued my interest.

"If you like this," Bubba said, "let me show you all the stuff in the basement." And with that, we were off. We walked to the back of the store and down a few steps into a veritable vault. Everywhere I looked, shelves brimmed with pharmaceutical paraphernalia, all of which reinforced the idea that I was standing in an archive of medical relics.

There were old Randolph Prescription file boxes. There were old curative signs. There were old medical magazines. There were old medicine bottles. And there was much, much more. As we walked about the basement, Bubba talked about the numerous donations of old pharmacy treasures he had made to a local university for its medical collection. That tidbit of information confirmed the feeling I had already formed about this place and Bubba, that both housed benevolent spirits.

Bubba's return to work was inevitable, and all too soon I had to follow him back up the stairs and into the drugstore. Seeing that the activity at Citizen's Pharmacy was kicking into high gear, I paid my tab, thanked everyone for their time, and once again found myself a traveler upon Brenham's streets of antiquity.

Citizens Pharmacy
201 E. Main
Brenham, TX 77833
(409) 836-3651

Citizens Pharmacy

Randermann's

RANDERMANN'S

After having the good fortune to find a pharmacy with a soda fountain in downtown Brenham, Mark and I ventured out to see what the countryside might turn up. We headed north on State Highway 105 and soon discovered a small, white building with red trim that looked like it had once been a service station and a store. Even though the old gas pumps were gone, I commented that the cars scattered about the store's front indicated the possibility that Randermann's might be a gathering spot.

Walking to the front door, I glanced about and noticed two outhouses set back fifty feet from the building. An old coon dog lying in the bed of a truck peered over the tailgate, sniffed the air, then dropped his droopy face to resume his doggie dreams.

Everybody inside Randermann's—without missing a syllable in their easy exchanges—looked up at me as I entered through the screen door. Two men sat at a game board in front of the window, two more men sat at a spot near the middle of the room, and three women sat at a tall, round table in the far right corner of the store. I pulled up a chair to the blue Formica table and watched the slender woman with a bobbed haircut.

As she walked over to get my order, I looked about the room and admired the modest decor. A few shelves stocked with grocery items lined the front right wall. Midway down the room's right side a pot-bellied wood stove and two chairs stood directly in front of a closed door. Beyond that, a small black-and-white dog lounged in a halo of sun rays that shone upon a vinyl couch pushed into the far right corner.

Along the back wall another door stood ajar and invited a cross breeze to enter. The room's left section housed an old refrigerator which squared up with a tall counter; together they marked off the kitchen area. On one end of the counter, a vase that held Texas bluebells ignited a spark of color that fused with the room's green hues. An antique cash register—still used to ring up sales—sat at the counter's other end.

The distant hissing of cars passing in front of the store worked in concert with the muted whispering of ceiling fans that revolved overhead. No distracting music or television played; it was just us and the place and our thoughts.

When I asked to whom I should speak to get some information about the store, everyone—in a synchronized motion—flipped a thumb toward Lorena Randermann, the graceful lady who had greeted me when I first entered.

In a sociable yet spunky style, Mrs. Randermann shared the store's history, interjecting it with humorous memories to which everyone present seemed privy. In 1956 she and her husband, Henry, built the store and gas station, and since then the only structural change that has occurred is

when they removed the old gas pumps. She even pointed out that they still use the original outhouses.

As Lorena spoke about her husband's death in 1980, the white dog, Saucie—who has since passed away—ambled over and she reached down to pet him. Within seconds, her black-and-white dog, Nubbin, also trotted over for some attention. Shortly Lorena looked at her watch and announced that she had work to tend to up at the house, so she said Dallas and Buddy could continue where she had left off.

Before they broke into their recollections, Dallas walked behind the counter, brought out a jar of canned pickles, and opened it. Both men grabbed a pickle, crunched a bite, and started their stories of the annual 4th of July barbecues, the games of pitch in the winter, and the days of playing volleyball outside. They munched on the pickles and remembered the many card games and the day twenty years ago when the jukebox was taken out. With pride, they explained that this place is their neighborly stomping grounds, and as they talked their respect and fondness for Lorena continuously surfaced.

I learned that Floyd, the man sitting at the table by the front window, has worked for Lorena since he was fourteen or fifteen. He is over sixty years old now. As they jabbered away, Nelda Henze, who had also worked for Mrs. Randermann for many years, whirled in through the back door and joined the conversation. For more than an hour these longtime regulars graciously shared their sweep of memories with me.

All too soon it was time to hit the road. As I stepped outside and the screen door slapped behind me, the old coon dog raised his head and followed me with his onyx eyes. I scribbled into my journal that every dog has his day, and apparently I had just had mine at Randermann's where life flows slowly and easily.

Randermann's
Hwy 105
Brenham, TX 77833
(409) 836-8565

Randermann's

SCHOLZ GARTEN

Around eleven o'clock in the morning, we headed to downtown Austin under pewter clouds patched with blue sky that created a canopy-like cover overhead. KGSR, a local radio station, wafted its eclectic music mix as we wove through one-way streets to San Jacinto Boulevard where construction of nearby high-rise parking garages dwarfed a single-story historical beer garden. We parked, put quarters into the meter, and strode toward Scholz Garten.

The simple elegance of the corner building's sandy-beach and barn-red bricks offered a calm facade under the tin-roofed porch that sheltered me from drizzling rain. Once inside, I was engulfed by a lunchtime crowd whose enthusiastic voices bounced off the room's wood floor and ceiling, swamping the space with energy. The closely spaced tables were filled so I took a seat at the counter made of teak, pine, and redwood, which dated back to the late 1800s. Below the glow of lights and neon signs, its dark surface glistened with muted colors. The back bar, constructed of the same materials, displayed a mirror that ran the counter's length and allowed a full view of the room and its patrons.

A mural at the back bar's front, right end offered a peek at the talent of a local muralist, Dr. Norman, whose work at one time had covered most of the restaurant's walls. Since much of his work has been painted over, the present owner is making great efforts to uncover those scenes and bring them back to life. I learned that Jesse Kinser, a waitress at the restaurant for over twenty years, also helped with the paintings.

I walked about the room and checked out the items on the walls. Light streaming in through wood blinds on one of the four front windows cast slatted lines onto a nearby table as I viewed a framed handbill advertising a vocal and instrumental concert held at Scholz on February 24, 1871. Other framed items chronicled a one-hundred-thirty-six-year lifetime of both Scholz Garten and Austin scenes.

A slanted walkway led into a dining room added in the 1970s, which offered a setup for large parties and banquet-style events. I walked back into the front room then down into an area referred to as the Bismarck Room that was built onto the original structure over ninety years ago. It held tables and booths filled with patrons. An array of framed handbills touting musicians and bands that had played at the old Armadillo Headquarters hung on one wall, and upon another I noted a lamp that highlighted a small mural, signed by both Dr. Norman and Ms. Kinser, that depicted the Alamo.

Then I headed out the back doors, which opened onto a spacious patio. The pewter clouds had disappeared, allowing the sun's rays to filter through the branches of seven grand elm and pecan trees that created a natural ceiling over a handful of customers sitting at picnic tables and enjoying the slight breeze. I

took a seat at a table that provided a clear view of a stage whose pastoral mural depicted a German-style beer garden with mountains in the background. Just as I snapped a photo of this artwork, a voice interjected, "That was painted by an art teacher at a local community college." I turned and met the current beer garden manager, Tom Davis.

He invited me to sit with him as he eagerly talked about August Scholz, a German immigrant, who had built the original bar and cafe in 1866 and had added other sections as need arose. Mr. Scholz ran the place until his death in 1891, at which time his stepson took over for two years before selling the business to the Lemp Brewery Company in 1893. Later, in 1908, a German singing club, the Austin Saengerrunde, purchased the business and built a hall and six-lane bowling alley next door—both are in operation today. The Saengerrunde stills owns Scholz Garten; however, they have leased the bar and restaurant to various people over the years, with the latest being Tom Davis, who began his lease in 1996.

Tom expressed his loyalty to maintaining the German heritage of this historical landmark that has served a wide range of clientele—from University of Texas students and supporters to local citizens to Texas politicos. He then remarked how the 1966 Texas legislature had honored Scholz Garten as "a gathering place for Texans of discernment, taste, culture, erudition" and how it "epitomized the finest tradition of magnificent German heritage."

When asked about the changes Tom said, "A lot of the patrons used to be oil men and land people, but now the crowds represent more of a cross section." Then in a quieter voice he reminisced about the days when one was able to see the State Capitol's dome from the restaurant's front door. I commented that this establishment, which has existed since 1866, is proof that some businesses can endure throughout the years. Shortly after my last statement I thanked Mr. Davis for his time, and he returned to hanging a newly painted sign.

When I reached the gate to the street, I glanced back once again to view the beauty of this place that had resulted from August Scholz' vision, and I realized that despite the surrounding mountainous structures of concrete and steel, the spirit and soul of Scholz Garten would be here long after those other buildings had crumbled under the hands of time.

Scholz Garten
1607 San Jacinto Boulevard
Austin, TX 78701
(512) 474-1958

Scholz Garten

Scholz Garten

KNEBEL'S TAVERN

We took Interstate 35 around 3 o'clock in the afternoon in order to miss the heavy traffic and drove north until we hooked up with Farm Road 1825 at the Pflugerville exit. Despite growth about the area, the road curved through relatively open land until we hit Pecan Street where traffic snarled on the two-lane road; I slowed my pace.

Then as we scanned the street a flapping American flag and six pickup trucks signaled our arrival at Knebel's Tavern.

On the outside wall, red letters advertised Ed's Barbecue on Friday and Saturday from 7 A.M. until ?

I stepped from daylight into dark, and once my eyes adjusted I observed six customers at a table near the back and two at the counter. I joined the counter patrons, ordered a beer, and soon learned that this twenty-eight-foot, antique mahogany counter had been the result of a trade between Moody Anderson, a collector of relics since way back, and the tavern's owner, Tuffy Knebel. Seems Moody traded this one for another counter that had stood in the old place.

The back bar boiled over with knick-knacks. There was a picture of a young Willie Nelson, a stuffed eight-point deer head, longhorn antlers, a radio, two old brass cash registers, two new cash registers, a television atop a soda refrigerator, and too many other items to list.

I walked about the warehouse-style room filled with tables, neon signs, old metal advertising signs, and snapshots on a bulletin board. Christmas lights and a Christmas tree cast a festive spirit about the place year round. Beer boxes were stacked seven feet high against one wall where nearby video games waited to be played. Another wall displayed two old maps that hung not far from a frame with photos and names of local military men who had served during World War II. This frame of honor, according to the owner, was salvaged from the old Austin 7-Up Bottling Company.

After I returned to the counter, a patron strolled over, and soon I was visiting with Wayne, who described himself as an "old hippie from hell," born and reared in Austin, and an army soldier during the Vietnam War.

Ed Driska then joined us and started chatting about the tavern and how he used to help "Big Daddy," who for years had provided the barbecue for Knebel's Tavern. But when "Big Daddy" died twelve years ago, Ed stepped in and took over the barbecue business. Although he is at the place almost every day, Ed clarified that he "sells his fixings" on Fridays and Saturdays. And sell it he does as evidenced by the weekly, two-day averages: three hundred pounds of brisket, one hundred and fifty pounds of sausage, and sixty pounds of pork ribs. He has seen his business grow as technology companies have moved into

Knebel's Tavern

the area, so he just keeps serving them "until he runs out." When I asked about the tavern's history, he said I'd have to wait until Tuffy came in.

That wait allowed me to talk with another regular, Louis Zbranek—a retired, thirty-two-year Maytag repairman—who filled me in on Knebel's old-timers, a group of men in their seventies and eighties who have lived in Pflugerville all their lives. They come in every day around 3:30 P.M. and sit at the long table with the blue office chairs. Louis pointed to the sign above the table that read, Board Room. "That's where they meet and discuss life." Then he named those at the table this day—Alfred, Robert, Hub, and Kenny. Next Louis talked about the Breakfast Club that gathers three or four weekday mornings around eight to cook and eat breakfast. "We kind of take care of each other," Louis explained as he rattled off a few names, "There's Howard, B.R., Morris, Telephone Bob, Joe P., Wayne, Ed, and me."

"Tuffy's here," hollered Ed. As I looked up, Burwell "Tuffy" Knebel walked toward me sipping on a bottled Coca-Cola. Since this man didn't look so "tough," I asked about his nickname. "I guess I never cried when I was a kid," he chuckled, "so the other guys just gave me that name."

Tuffy Knebel, born December 19, 1923, at the old St. David's Hospital in Austin, has lived in the area all of his life. After high school, he served in the navy during World War II for thirty-seven months and three days. "Yep," he said, "I got out of the navy on the thirteenth, drunk on the fourteenth, and went to work for my dad on the fifteenth."

His dad's business, a confectionery and tailor shop, was housed on Main Street, but after his dad's death in 1952, Tuffy took over and moved four years later to a building on Pecan Street; that site now houses a Lawn and Repair Shop. Twenty-seven years later, in 1983, he moved to the present location. "Yeah," he mused as he shot me a smile and took a sip of his soda, "I moved about a block in fifty-two years." Tuffy works seven days a week, but since he doesn't get up as early as he used to, he now arrives in the afternoon and stays until midnight. Not bad for a man who last year celebrated his seventy-fifth birthday at the tavern with a polka band from Ranger and free food for all his guests.

When I asked what he liked best about his business, he didn't hesitate. "The people," he said. "I'm going to get a sign made that says, 'Through these doors pass the world's greatest people—our customers.'" Here was a man stout of character who offered a solid business in order for people to have a place to gather and experience a sense of camaraderie.

Knebel's Tavern
109 E. Pecan Street
Pflugerville, TX 78691
(512) 251-4129

Knebel's Tavern

Knebel's Tavern

Charlie's Bar-B-Q

CHARLIE'S BAR-B-Q

State Highway 71 East served as the artery out of Austin as we left Oak Hill around 9:45 A.M. The morning rush hour had thinned, yet traffic remained thick until State Highway 304 South where we headed to Rosanky. Oak trees lined the two-lane road and shimmered with sunlight.

Continuing east on Farm Road 535 and on into Smithville, a drive down Main Street revealed only a few open establishments. Then we spied a building near the railroad tracks; its sign announced Charlie's Bar-B-Q.

I made a U-turn and pulled up in front of a fire-engine red brick building with taxi-cab yellow doors and window frames. The aroma of pit-smoked barbecue sent my taste buds hopping like water on hot grease. I checked my watch, 10:42 A.M. "Oh well," I uttered, "close enough to lunch time."

With the screen door closed behind me the large, boxy room felt cozy, a factor attributed to the red tin ceiling. Two pipes, like widely spaced train tracks, ran along the ceiling and held eight fans that kicked up a breeze and cooled the heat of indoor pits. Throughout the room, fifteen tables with red plastic tablecloths were surrounded by red-and-yellow metal folding chairs, and upon each table was BBQ sauce and a roll of paper towels—a sign of some finger-licking food.

Three customers savored their food as I strolled to the waist-high red counter and waited for the petite woman to finish her work. When she saw me, she moved over to the register. "What can I get you?" Virginia Ebner asked. I stepped back, looked up at the menu board, and ordered. She lifted meat from the warmer, placed it on a scale, weighed it, then plopped it on a plate. After I selected side orders, she rang up the bill and passed the red plastic tray to me.

As I ate, I studied the room. Sunlight, slanting through small windows high on the wall, added to the airiness created by large plate-glass windows and screen doors. An American flag leaned against a window frame, a Norfolk pine towered in one corner, and a heater stood against a wall. A guitar, prints, articles, and the ever-present hunter's symbol—a stuffed deer head—adorned the walls. In a corner stood an old upright piano and down the wall hung a long mirror.

By 11 o'clock, six people stood in a single line that stretched back from the counter where Charlie Ebner greeted them with a sheepish grin, took their order, weighed it, and made certain they were satisfied.

Charlie called out the price to his wife, Virginia, who stood at the nearby register. The customer would then sidle over and answer Virginia's clipped questions: "Onions or pickles? Bread or chips? What to drink?" She placed the requests onto a

Charlie's Bar-B-Q

tray, rang up the bill, and slid the tray across the counter. Even as the room filled, voices remained soft and pliable amid the celing fans' whirrings, only to be interrupted by banging screen doors as they snapped shut.

Virginia couldn't give the count for daily customers, but she pointed out that they just "keep coming in all day long." Then she gestured toward the store's front and said, "Sometimes we'll have them lined up clear to the door." I eyeballed the distance—twenty or more feet—then turned my attention to the patient customers talking with the Ebners. While some got meals to go, most dined in, and everyone cleaned up after themselves.

Charlie traced the history to 1908 when the Polanski family built Polanski's BBQ. They ran it until 1946 when Charlie and Emma Ebner (Charlie's parents) bought it and changed the name to Charlie's Bar-B-Q. They owned it for fourteen years, then Mike Mikeska took over from 1960 to 1980, during which time Charlie Jr. worked for him. When the building's rear portion burned in 1963, Mr. Mikeska and Charlie built a new addition and added indoor pits. In 1980 Charlie became owner and has kept the fires burning and customers content since.

Charlie grinned over at Virginia and announced, "It's just the two of us. We're chief cooks and bottle washers. And we make everything from scratch." And they do this fifty-one weeks a year, six days a week, Monday through Saturday from 8 A.M. until 4 P.M.

As I listened, I noticed Virginia had filled bowls with cobbler and ice cream and was carrying them to customers, yet I never heard anyone order the treat. When I asked about this, Virginia filled another bowl, handed it to me, and said, "Enjoy! It's Free Dessert Tuesday." And enjoy it I did.

After two hours it was time to continue the search for another treasure. I thanked the Ebners for their hospitality and good food, and as Charlie wiped his hands on his apron he pointed out that at one time Smithville had seven grocery stores on Main Street and every one of them made a little living, but now the town only has two big stores. "I've been blessed," he offered humbly, "because our place has been a tradition for over fifty-three years."

I mused that traditions are simply not doled out, but rather earned through strong beliefs and good people. And Smithville is fortunate that Charlie's Bar-B-Q and the people behind its success have stood the tests of tradition.

Charlie's Bar-B-Q
110 Main Street
Smithville, TX 78957
(512) 237-3317

Charlie's Bar-B-Q

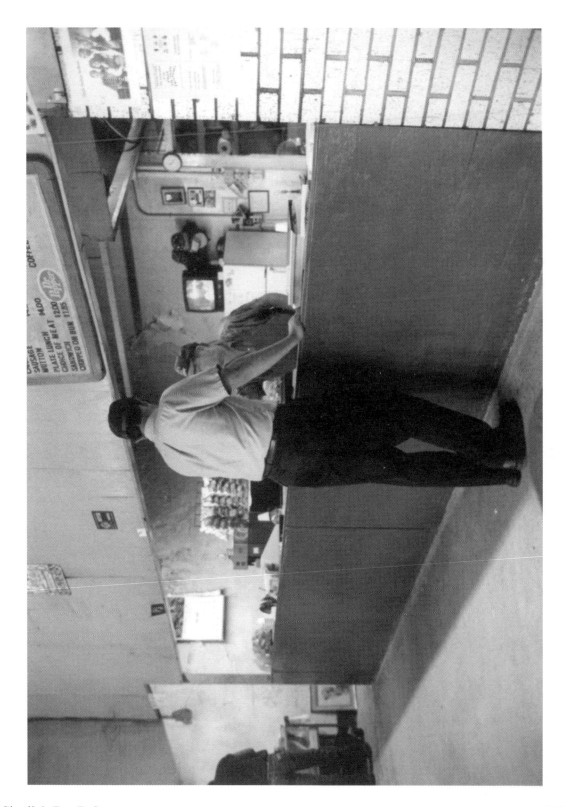

Charlie's Bar-B-Q

PAVLAS TAVERN

We left Charlie's Bar-B-Q in Smithville some time after one in the afternoon and took State Highway 95 South. A place in Winchester didn't pan out so we zig-zagged on a southwesterly course, eventually passing through Luling. From there a southeasterly jaunt led to Farm Road 532 and into Moulton. We slowed to check out the business area that sat on a hill above the railroad tracks and decided to stop, a decision that proved wise as we soon discovered Pavlas Tavern on Main Street.

I parked in front of a string of connected businesses, and when I stepped out of the truck a hush enveloped the area as clouded, gray skies muffled the air. I strode up five steep steps to the sidewalk that led to the tavern. No one walked about, but this mid-afternoon lull in activity had been typical of many small towns during the trips. I peered through a window into the darkened bar but couldn't make out any distinctive features, so I reached for the low handle on the heavy wood door, depressed the latch, and entered. A duskiness imbued the room, yet somehow the dimness fit the ambiance of this stately place whose wood floor chronicled a collective sense of history and time.

First to catch my attention were the 1950s-style Formica tables—one pink, one yellow with star bursts, and one blue-and-white—that sat about the front. A red couch, also from the fifties, offered a cozy spot for customers. These "modern" pieces of furniture were subtle contrasts to the aged, elegant cypress bar and back bar that stretched down the room.

I seemed alone, but as I started to sit at a table, the office door on my left opened and out strolled George Pavlas. He nodded his head, crossed my path, and walked behind the counter. When he pulled up a stool, I moved over to the bar and sat at one of the six wood barstools bolted to the floor, and with an introduction, Mr. Pavlas extended a firm handshake that spoke of security, of confidence. I noted his white, crisply pressed, pin-striped shirt and his gray polyester pants.

Although two types of draught beer were available, I opted for a soda and relaxed under the turning ceiling fans as George talked. He pointed out the twenty-foot tin ceiling which had originally been painted white but now is amber from years of cigar and cigarette smoke. This site had once housed a wood structure, also a tavern, prior to a fire in 1922. After it burned down, the bar was rebuilt by Mr. Charles Luecke and remained in his and Mrs. Luecke's hands until around 1960 when George Pavlas and his wife, Vlasta, bought it.

With a glint in his eye, he explained it was natural for them to run the business because after falling in love with Vlasta at a Schulenburg football game, George had known they would spend their lives together. So together they have kept it going for almost forty years, and during those years very little about the decor and structure has changed. He pointed out that

Pavlas Tavern

the three counters in the bar had once been scattered about the room, but to create a continuous row of counter space the Pavlas had moved them to all face the side wall. First there was the cypress counter with its barstools, then the Formica-topped counter with its four freestanding stools, and last the L-shaped oak counter, which didn't offer seating. Their varying heights formed a stair-stepped "counter scape."

The tavern's back section seemed even more expansive than the front. It held tables for all sizes of gatherings and a pool table for those who wished to play a quick game. Along one wall stood a jukebox that offered country and western selections.

When I noticed a recessed area in the ceiling, George explained it was originally a skylight, but after he and Vlasta bought the place they had installed an attic fan to help cool the room. As if he anticipated my next question, George walked over and turned a switch. With a clunk and a whoosh, the fan's outer blinds opened, and I watched as the rotation of the fan's blades flashed psychedelic sun rays onto the floor. Then, just as quickly as the fan had come to life, George turned the switch and the blades stopped, the blinds shut, and the interior returned to dusk.

George had gone back to his place behind the counter and I to my stool when a customer entered and struck up a conversation with him. As they chatted, I noted the large, amber-colored glass chandeliers that hung overhead, and then I studied the back bar. Plastic spruce garland stretched along its top and fronted a Christmas vignette that displayed miniature forms and structures. Located at the top and middle of the back bar was an old Lone Star clock that I later learned had only been repaired once in all its days, and that repair had involved a good oiling with W-D 40; the clock has kept perfect time since.

Two signs amongst the many on the back bar and wall tickled my fancy. One asked the question, "Do you want to talk to the one in charge or the one who knows what's going on?" and the other read, "Women's faults are many. Men have only two, Everything they say and Everything they do." As I laughed aloud, the two men looked my way.

With that, George took a black-and-white framed photo from off the back bar and handed it to me. I found myself looking at George and Vlasta, both younger, standing like proud owners before the old back bar. George explained that through the twenty-five years he worked for Alcoa, Vlasta often had to run the business alone.

There was pride in his tone, then that tone grew even richer when he talked of their three beautiful daughters.

As he took the photo from me and returned it to its place, I studied his broad shoulders and his firm hands and sensed that not only had life been good to George Pavlas, but he had been good to life.

Pavlas Tavern
P.O. Box 225
Moulton, TX 77975
(never had a phone)

RED ROCK GENERAL STORE

Late one evening we followed a lead to Red Rock expecting to peer through darkened windows. However, once Farm Road 20 rounded a gentle curve, bright neon signs emanated in the twilight, so we hopped out of the truck and skipped up the steps to meet John Pilot, a man with a peaceful demeanor, whose mother owns the store. He suggested a return the next day to talk with her, so return we did to the Red Rock General Store.

At 9 A.M. the trip down State Highway 71 began under clear skies, then at U.S. 183 I headed east to Farm Road 812. As I sped away from the main road, luscious pecan and wispy mesquite trees accented by sunflowers painted the vista along the country road.

Five buildings on Main Street marked the downtown area, but the Red Rock General Store loomed high above them all. Its five broad concrete steps climbed up to a deep porch supported by cedar posts. I opened the green wood door and stepped inside. The sweet smell of hay filled the room as I looked upward at the old tin ceiling painted white. Straight ahead, a U-shaped counter revealed evidence of wear and tear along its green top, and from behind it a petite woman talked with a customer. When the customer left she turned, "Are you the lady from Austin?" I nodded and began my exchange with Tracy Hill, the owner's daughter.

Tracy explained that she and her brother share the workload with their mother. "People in these parts," Tracy commented, "leave early and get home late so we have to be here for them." Red Rock General Store is open from 5:30 A.M. until 10:30 P.M.

As I waited for Tracy's mom to arrive, I studied the store, first noting the single shopping cart. Lining each side wall were shelves filled with sundry merchandise, and atop them was an array of antiques. In the middle section, coolers held soft drinks and perishables, and over to the right, stacks of feed and racks of breads and pastries filled the space.

At the store's front, photos and articles hung on the wall. One photo portrayed Red Rock in July of 1927, and another offered a view of Main Street. One article highlighted Dunc Lentz, but the most intriguing item was a small frame that held a Lentz coin and the handwritten note, "Compliments of Todd Voight."

I turned as the door opened and in walked Myrna Bushnell, who extended her hand in welcome then gestured for me to pull up a stool. "My late husband's greatest pleasure," she offered, "was sitting on that stool and talking to everybody when they came in."

She explained that she and her husband Don—who died only a month before my visit—had moved from Austin to Red Rock years ago. "This store," she said, "just talked to me. It needed somebody to love it so I told Don I wanted to buy it when it

Red Rock General Store

came up for sale." Don held out for a while then one day told her they could give it a shot, and that began their connection to this legendary place. They bought the structure in May of 1996 and, with "a community who rallied behind" them, reopened its doors on June 15, 1996.

Myrna pointed out that the six original counters were moved around and fresh coats of paint applied to the store's tile bricks poured right here in Red Rock by Mr. Lentz. Air conditioning was also installed, but Myrna's desire to maintain authenticity led to her steadfast refusal for putting in a drop ceiling. We then walked to the back and into another large room. Like a little girl with a secret, Myrna leaned forward and uttered, "They used to sell coffins out of this room in the old days."

Myrna traced the store's history to the Pester Mercantile Company built in 1868 by William Pester, who moved it to this location in 1892. In 1904 O. B. Lentz bought the business, renaming it O. B. Lentz Company, but watched his investment burn in the 1918 town fire. He rebuilt and two years later turned the management over to his son Dunc, with whom he watched as the place again burned. In 1948 Dunc bought the establishment and ran it until his death in 1991. Then Stuart Hershap took over until 1994 when Kathleen Stevens assumed ownership; she sold the business to Don and Myrna in 1996.

I asked about the framed Lentz coin, and Myrna explained, "Mr. Lentz took care of the people. He made his own money during the Depression, and when locals bought from or traded with him he gave them change with his coins. That way they could always come back and get what they needed to make it."

The door then opened and in walked Russell Smith, who has worked at the store for over a year. After introductions, he and I strolled next door to the adjacent structure. The sixty-foot room smelled like a barn. Bales of hay stacked up about seven feet high ran along the left wall, and a variety of feed sacks filled the room's middle and right sections. Plaster walls had fallen away in spots to reveal the same tile brick used for the store. Russell then pointed to an oval-shaped painting on the wall and shared the story of the hungry vagrant who had come to town during the Depression without a dime to his name. So Mr. Lentz struck up a deal with him, and in exchange for this landscape picture he provided the out-of-towner work and food.

After returning to the store, I bid my thanks but just as I opened the door to leave, Russell chimed up, "If you like this place, you ought to head over to Leon's Country Store in Rockne." Since the suggestions of locals had proven my best leads, I pulled back the heavy door, stepped onto the porch, and headed to Leon's place.

Red Rock General Store
201 Main Street
Red Rock, TX 78662
(512) 321-3360

Leon's Country Store

LEON'S COUNTRY STORE

We took Farm Road 20 to Rockne then turned right at Farm Road 535 and found a wooden building that stood like a small outpost. We pulled onto the gravel lot and parked under an oak tree whose umbrella-like branches protected us from the glaring sun. A large beer truck braked to a stop and sent dust swirling as we headed toward the store. Once inside, the noon heat was displaced by chilled air, and directly behind us the delivery man wheeled in an order of beer for Leon's Country Store.

A pretty woman with brown hair turned fawn-like eyes toward me and smiled. With liquid movements she examined some paperwork and wrote a check for the beer. When she had time, I explained why I had stopped, but before she could comment, the front door flew open and another hand truck stacked with beer cases rattled in.

As Lea Ann Goertz took care of business, I moseyed about the store noticing that everywhere I looked mementos sang of a lively existence. Snapshots on the walls invited a glimpse of patrons; amid them were signs, old Christmas cards, an American flag, and a collection of beer bottles that stood like silent monuments in a shrine. The wood floor creaked underfoot.

I perched on an old bench and turned to the gentleman sitting in a chair beside me; his posture was tall and proud. Carefully, eighty-eight-year-old Nat Hernandez moved the cane leaning against his chair, shook my hand, then explained his thirty-year patronage to the store. Using his cane for support, he rose and led me over to a picture that hung on the wall. "They're my beautiful granddaughters, Lilly and Christina," beamed this burly, silver-haired man before returning to his chair.

The door opened and in walked Russell Smith from the Red Rock store. When he saw me, a grin danced across his face and he said, "Told you this was a good place to check out."

Russell struck up a conversation with Nat, so I sketched the counter with its slanted V shape that jutted out slightly and formed a corner with another counter. Its white porcelain top was worn, and above it, parallel to the ceiling, hung the store's most eclectic memento—a mannequin leg flaunting fish net hose and a funky retro high heel.

I walked through a short hallway and found a room where a pool table fronted a jukebox adorned with its own mascot, a bumpy-skinned plastic frog. A couple of tables stood at the side with signs boasting "Texas Size Taste" and "True to Texas," while above an office door, the words "Sit Long—Talk Much" fit this local hangout.

Then I turned my attention to the bar. Quite utilitarian, the owners had doubled the beer cooler's use by filling it with drinks and letting it serve as the counter. License plates hung on the wall alongside a cow skull, a stuffed baby alligator, and a headless, stuffed snake skin. I then rejoined

Leon's Country Store

the others in the store—Lea Ann, Nat, Russell, a delivery man, another customer, and "B" the short-haired house dog.

The door opened again and in walked Frederick Goertz, who traced the store's history beginning with William Hilbig and his son Fred who sometime after the turn of the century built the place and named it William Hilbig and Son. Then Frederick's lifelong friend Leon Goertz took over the business in 1969 and renamed it Leon's Country Store. Frederick grew pensive as he recalled Leon's untimely death in 1990, then brightened as he explained that Herman, one of Leon's sons, had stepped in seventeen years ago to run the place. Lea Ann, Leon's daughter, manages the store while his son Jimmy takes care of the hog business.

For the fifteenth time, the door opened and Lea Ann introduced me to her brother Herman. The two recalled how their father had worked and played hard and made friends all over, so after his death they never questioned their family roles. Herman offered that he'd grown up in Rockne and that he "wouldn't ever think about growing up anywhere else." He said he did a little bit of everything, but his "memories of the store and Rockne were all good."

Lea Ann boasted about her brother's yearly 4th of July community fireworks show and about his house band, The Roadhouse Dogs. He grinned then added, "This store is kind of like our living room where we all gather up."

With that, Lea Ann introduced me to her boyfriend, Wayne "The Train" Hancock, who took a puff on his skinny cigar, tipped his head, then with a quick, firm handshake befitting his spunky nature talked about the juke joint swing that his band plays. Just then, Wayne's music jumped into the room from the jukebox, and he and Lea Ann exchanged elfin smiles.

Once more, the door flew open and in walked Karla Nichols whose warm smile and gentle demeanor made her instantly likable. Karla spoke of her eight-and-one-half-year relationship with Leon before his death, then in her lilting, child-like voice proclaimed the store to be her "second home where everyone is happy and caring."

As Karla left, I asked Lea Ann to comment on the family business. After taking a sip of her Big Red she said, "My favorite thing about the store is that the people who come here span all walks of life, all races, and all ages."

Enough said. This statement proved that Leon Goertz had reared children with big hearts. As I left, I read a sign that asked, "Have You Hugged Your Bubba Today," and knew that today I indeed had been hugged by Leon's spirit that lives on through his family.

Leon's Country Store
Route 1 Box 109
Bastrop, TX 78602
(512) 321-7346

Leon's Country Store

Blanco Bowling Club Cafe

BLANCO BOWLING CLUB CAFE

After the hopping activity at Leon's Country Store, we drove to Austin, took U.S. 290 West, and cruised through Oak Hill. After that, the country became a rural ocean of swells that frothed with cedar, mesquite, and oak trees and splashed with new subdivisions and businesses—reminders of urban sprawl. At the junction of U.S. 290 and U.S. 281, a southerly turn provided a roller coaster ride into Blanco, and near the destination, rain clouds gathered and the temperature dropped. In town, no one hurried. At Fourth Street we turned left, drove past the old courthouse, and pulled alongside two trucks parked in front of the Blanco Bowling Club Cafe.

I stepped from my truck just as a man and his family strolled up a ramp leading to the cafe's vestibule. I mirrored their entry by using the walk on the opposite side of the lobby.

I stood at the doorway, then following the welcome from a waitress behind the food counter, I took a seat at one of six barstools. I spoke with Barbara Nolte, a gregarious woman who juggled about eight jobs at once. Her friendly nature and willingness to listen won me over. As we chatted, Barbara filled tea glasses, grabbed sets of silverware, and loaded her arms with plates from the kitchen's serving window. And she never missed a stride.

From my vantage point, I observed the cooks as they scurried about the kitchen, then I noticed the pies. These sumptuous treats, a dessert lover's delight, flaunted a meringue that reached like miniature golden mountains to a height of about four or five inches. Before long I met Barbara's daughter Melody and watched this mother and daughter team sidestep each other like a choreographed dancing duo. I saw them scribble down orders, snap tickets onto the round ticket holder in the serving window, spin the holder toward the cooks, and turn to the next customer.

Dizzy from their actions, I twirled around and studied the modest 1960s-style decor of the dining area whose walls displayed oil paintings of rural scenes. A jukebox, buffet cart, and rest rooms were located along the opposite wall; fourteen tables, each topped with the same wood-grain Formica laminate as the counter, provided seating. Along one wall, two doors led into another room so I slipped off the stool, peeked through one of the doorways, and was rewarded with a sweet sight for snooping eyes.

Inside the low-lit room I stood transfixed, staring at a quaint, six-lane, nine-pin bowling alley where scoring tables set up at each pair of lanes were straight out of the early fifties. A rack filled with bowling balls of different sizes, trophies in a glass cabinet, and blackboards on the walls provided ample evidence that this was a happening place. Then I noticed a man and woman playing dominoes at one of the twelve tables set up near the room's

Blanco Bowling Club Cafe

bar. I returned to the cafe and waited for a break in Barbara's routine.

Before long I met Virgie McHugh, who had just finished her game of dominoes. Virgie, who had been a waitress at the cafe for six years and served as the day manager for the last three years, took the stool next to me and with a pleasant attitude talked about the early-morning domino regulars who have been coming in "forever." But to explain the changes at the cafe, Virgie simply smiled and offered that the place has pretty much stayed the same. "If you've got something working," she said, "you don't want to change it."

With these words, a man stepped up to the counter's end and waited for a pause in our discourse. At the first break, I met John L. Dechert, current manager and president of the Blanco Bowling Club. Virgie rose and John took her seat and soon shared the history of the place.

First, he explained that the cafe and club are not owned and run by any one person, but rather by the Blanco Bowling Club members and its Board of Directors. However, he was quick to add that it wasn't always set up in this fashion. Back in 1948 when the place was first built, Roland Binseil owned the business. Then throughout the years ownership had fallen into many hands. There was Elmer Schwab from 1956 to 1958, Fred and Evelyn Wagenfehr from 1958 to 1965, and C. A. and Florence Weeaks from 1965 to 1967. In 1967, when a nearby nine-pin bowling alley burned, C.A. offered this establishment to them but they passed on the deal. At that time the members of the Blanco Bowling Club bought the business and pooled their energy and expertise to ensure a successful endeavor.

John, who has served as president of the club for the last thirteen years, stated it had been a "pretty good struggle at the beginning, but through the years everything has kind of fallen into place." He declared the success is due to the dedication of the club members and the community who have worked hard and supported efforts to make this a family place where kids and out-of-towners are always welcomed. He talked about the crowds that often fill both dining areas during the Friday catfish lunch specials and all-you-can-eat catfish dinners.

John then added he enjoys "being around people" and "it is the people that come in here that makes it such a good place to be." With my time at the Blanco Bowling Club Cafe at a close, I paid the tab and thanked everyone, and as I sat in the truck, I made a note to return one weeknight to eat a good meal and watch some stylish bowling.

Blanco Bowling Club Cafe
310 4th Street
Blanco, TX 78606
(830) 833-4416

Blanco Bowling Club Cafe

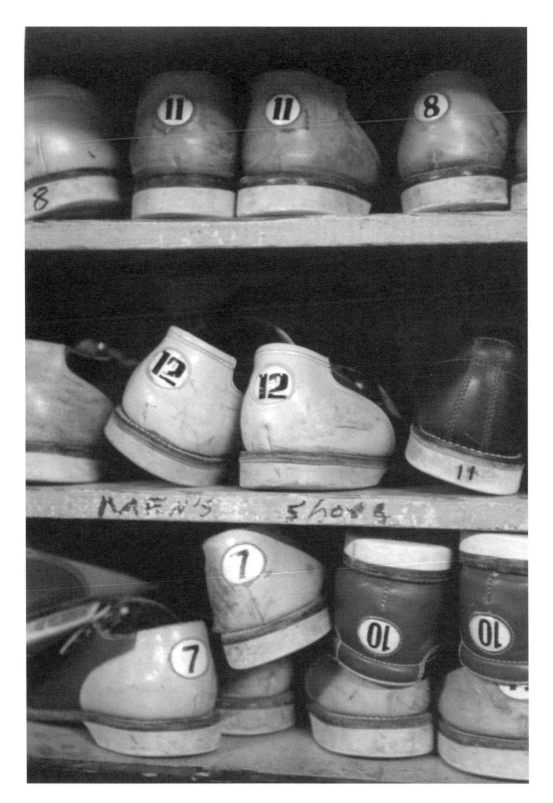

Bergheim General Store

BERGHEIM GENERAL STORE

At the Blanco Cafe, two employees suggested a jaunt south on U.S. 281 to State Highway 46 to check out some places. The first side trip was through Bulverde then on through luscious hill country to the west.

Cruising along, we spotted a limestone building, so I whipped the truck around and screeched to a halt in front of the structure we hoped would be a gold mine, and a gold mine the Bergheim General Store turned out to be.

I stood in the gravel lot sketching the next-door house then turned to the store's weathered limestone facade. The roof stair-stepped into a peak and held a sign that read, Bergheim General Store established in 1903.

I read the historical marker hanging on the outside wall and learned that the establishment's original name was the Engel Store, built by Andreas Engel who had moved to Texas from Austria via New York in 1885. In 1900 Mr. Engel purchased the land upon which the store sits, and in 1903 he and his wife, Eva, built the store. To this date it remains in the Engel family. Mr. Engel was credited with naming the new area Bergheim, German for "home in the hills," and looking around I found it a fitting name.

I started to enter but first eyed the limestone threshold that for almost a century had been graced by the footsteps of friends and customers. With reverence I placed my foot onto the stone's hollowed, swayed back that offered tell-tale signs of a long history, then I stepped inside.

Customers stood three deep at the old counter. The ruddy-faced man behind the counter called for help from a young man, and together they worked the two registers. The place buzzed with life.

Taking advantage of the bustle, I walked about the room, which held more merchandise per square inch than any other place I had seen. Everywhere I turned, my eyes were treated to all types, shapes, and sizes of items. Shelves that lined aisles barely wide enough to let two people pass overflowed with merchandise. On one side of the store were coolers, galvanized trash cans, and mailboxes. Cases of Kerr canning jars were there for the picking along with crock pots and kitchen utensils. And there was food—canned, bottled, boxed, and fresh—for any customer's needs. All of this took up only one third of the room.

I turned to the middle section that served as a clothing store. There were leather belts, work boots, and cowboy hats. There were hunting jump suits and flannel shirts. And there were T-shirts. A tall recessed cabinet at the back served as a shrine to yesteryear, so I rifled through the old jars, boxes, and cans with their faded labels. There was Regoes Cough Syrup for 30¢, Dutch Cleanser, Orium medicated salve, and Hofstra's Insect Powder.

Bergheim General Store

Then I turned my observations to the section that housed "something for everyone." There were pesticides, chains, video rentals, nails, wind chimes, gloves, and garden hoses. There were knives, plumbing hardware, school supplies, and pharmaceutical items.

There was an old brass cash register, circa 1903, that now sits idle. And there was an old McCaskey Account Register. I flipped through its metal registers noting the neatly penned names of past customers. Gingerly I opened its drawers and discovered handfuls of faded, yellowed papers. There were State of Texas store licenses for Mr. Alfred Engel dating back to the 1940s. There were old check stubs dating back to 1928. And there were old store tickets organized by year. I looked through ticket after ticket, noting the names of customers for whom the general store had been their lifeblood, and I marveled that three gallons of gas in 1928 cost 54¢.

At that point Vince Cooper, the young gentleman at the counter, came over and spent some time going through these relics and echoing my oohs and ahhs. Vince explained he is just "learning the inventory," but then confessed he didn't "think [he would] ever get it all down." A glance about the room led me to agree.

I then met the man in charge, Stanley Jones, whose ready smile quickened as I asked him to tell me about his connection to the store. He clarified that the original owner, Andreas Engel, was his great-grandfather. Andreas' son Alfred had fathered three daughters, and it was one of those daughters, Stanley's mother Genevieve, who stepped in to carry on the legacy; she passed the business on to her son. Stanley then showed me a book that traced the area's history, and with pride he turned to the pages honoring the Engels. While he helped a customer, I skimmed the material.

Moments later, Stanley showed me a small room at the store's front. As we entered this alcove, I noted a counter butted up against a closed door that, when opened, allowed customers to take care of postal business from the front porch. Next to the door were mailboxes that also opened onto the porch. Stanley confirmed his role as postmaster.

We walked back to his desk covered with stacks of ticket books, and he explained that like during the Depression the store still maintains personal credit for many of the locals. Then he walked over to the old counter, leaned on his hands, and recalled the many old-timers from the ranching community along with the farmers who are now gone. "But I'll keep this store here for those few old-timers who are still with us," he asserted, "and for the new folks moving into the area. I enjoy meeting all kinds of people, and many of the new people are becoming regular customers."

Bergheim General Store
843 Hwy 46 East
Bergheim, TX 78004
(830) 336-2112

Bergheim General Store

SEFCIK HALL

*On the suggestion of Moody Anderson—who since 1972 has owned
and refurbished The Grove, a western ghost town—we headed up I-35
North to check out an old dance hall. Trusting Moody's judgment, we
knew it more than likely would prove a winner, bringing my journeys
for this work to an end. As we turned east on State Highway 53 and
headed toward Seaton, little did we know that amid the infinite fields
of corn would be the Hope diamond of dance halls, Sefcik Hall.*

Once on Seaton Road, I spied the two-story, gently weathered structure whose metal-gray tin roof rose as a testament to time. The gravel parking lot was empty. A gentle breeze shushed through corn stalks as the drone of a distant tractor came and went.

A young girl poked her head out of the front door, smiled, then darted back inside. I gathered my gear and headed up the porch steps as a black dog sauntered around the corner, eyed me, then sat down. Pretty laid back place, I thought as I opened the screen door. Once inside, I blessed Moody for his suggestion.

To the right stood video games, tables, a jukebox, and three pool tables with overhead lights. Neon signs reflected off the white wall. A doorway at the back led to the kitchen from which came the clanging of pans and clacking of voices while in the far corner a television's clamor invaded the room's quietness.

Disregarding the noise, I absorbed the elegance of the twenty-foot mahogany counter with its steel foot rail and matching back bar whose mirror doubled the room's size. I placed my hands atop the counter's richly hued wood then heard, "It's over one hundred years old and it's from the old Buckhorn Saloon in Cameron." I turned and stared into the twinkling eyes of Alice Sulak, owner of Sefcik (pronounced Sheffchik) Hall. "It cost about $35," she continued. I traced the counter's thick, curved edge with its sheen from seventy-six years of customers leaning upon its handsome wood.

I sat down and invited Alice to join me, but she was canning pickles and said she'd have to turn me over to her granddaughter.

With that she called seven-year-old Shelby from the kitchen, and as quick as a summer storm this little hostess moved in. As I took notes, Shelby grabbed some paper, a pen, sat next to me, and also wrote. I copied the neon message above the back bar: "Sefcik Hall - Pearl - Since 1923," only to learn that for thirty years the sign had read "100% - Pearl - Since 1923"—that was before the 1950s when Mr. Sefcik started serving other beer brands. The mirror's hand-painted message read "Drink Hearty Folks and Remain Ladies and Gentlemen." Overhead, four antique lights with glass prisms glowed evanescent.

Shelby bounded across the room, I trailed her, and we headed to the outside doors at the building's front corner. She slid back the bolt, flung open the doors, and

led me up a stairway. As we stepped into the jet-black room, Alice called, "I'm coming up," so Shelby and I waited, and when Alice reached the landing she disappeared off to the left. I heard the first click, then the next, as the hall's shadows were transformed by the mellow glow from house lights.

Alice flipped one switch then another and that mellow glow gave way to a tent of fairy lights strung from side to side. "We put them up during the holidays," Alice explained, "and everybody asked us to leave them up." "Nice touch," I whispered. With that, Alice flipped on the house lights and left.

As Shelby ran about, I took notes. Along three walls, long alcoves with low, slanted ceilings held tables and chairs, and upon close inspection I noticed window coverings that when opened allowed wind to whip across the hall. After counting the posts fronting these recessed areas, I noted the oak tables and chairs around the perimeter. As I scuffled across the floor, I asked Shelby if it was new, and she recited, "Yes, it was put over the old floor in 1953 and my Grandma added air conditioning."

Shelby skipped over and hopped onto the stage. I followed and the two of us stood like performers before invisible faces. Noting the stage lights and rolled, painted canvas curtain overhead, I envisioned the musicians who had played at Sefcik Hall.

Downstairs Alice and Shelby's maternal grandmother, Rosie Wilde, joined us. Alice explained that her father, Tom Sefcik, had built the two-story general store and dance hall in 1923, and although the store had given way to a tavern, Tom and his wife, Tracy Motl Sefcik, had provided an enduring gathering spot for the Czech community. The Sefcik's two daughters, Adela and Alice, also became a big part of the place. When Alice was only ten years old, she played drums in her older sister's band, Adela and the Music Masters, and together they brought their musical spirit to the hall. Alice's passion for music has grown, and over the years she has added other instruments—the saxophone, keyboard, accordion, and trumpet—to her repertoire. Many Sunday evenings Alice plays in her house band, The Texas Heartbeats, as well as with Jerry Haisler and The Melody Five.

"One of the biggest parts of my life since I was ten," Alice shared, "has been music. After I became a single parent of three boys, anytime I got to playing music, I just sailed through the air." As her last words resonated, it was clear that destiny had blessed Alice Sulak with her music and Sefcik Hall.

Sefcik Hall
800 Seaton Road
Temple, TX 76501
(254) 985-2356

Sefcik Hall

Sefcik Hall

POSTSCRIPT

Through his words, Robert Frost—one of America's modern poets—captured the very essence, the very drama of life as we often know it. His eloquent and simplistic style served as a vehicle to honor the passing of life, a passing he often depicted through nature and the changing seasons. And Frost speaks to that passage with the poetic lines, "So dawn goes down to day. / Nothing gold can stay."

These ten simple words symbolically capture a truth that what is in the present may be gone from our touch tomorrow. Three of the places written about and photographed for this book—H & R Drugs in Hillsboro, Victoria Pharmacy in Victoria, and the Star Drug Store in Galveston—each have come to the end of their golden years as two of the places have closed their doors and one has burned to the ground. And this within the period of time it has taken to bring *Counter Culture Texas* to life.

While the passing of these businesses may evoke a sense of sadness, the decision to include them in this work is driven by the desire to bring a smile to your face as we honor their place in time. Perhaps the important message to heed is that we should seek out these treasures of Texas gold before the next "dawn goes down to day."

H & R DRUGS

When the Hillsboro courthouse fell victim to a massive fire—a disaster which served as a call to arms—local citizens and Texans from around the state joined together to return the historical building to its original grandeur. This restorative effort piqued my interest, so we traveled north from Austin along Interstate 35 to check things out. Little did we know that the initial reason for our travels would take a back seat to a treasure of a drugstore that we would find on the corner of N. Waco and Elm Street, H & R Drugs.

I walked inside this single-story building to find a clean and orderly store. The lady across the room looked up, I signaled that I didn't need any help, and she returned to unpacking boxes. Amid the room's quietness my attention turned to voices that filtered forward from the back right corner.

There I found an L-shaped soda fountain topped with pink Formica and lined with eight short barstools. Next to the counter were four booths with black-topped tables and army green benches. Four men sat in two of the booths, a lady sat at the counter, a gentleman stood at the fountain's far end, and integral to this picture was the tall woman who worked at the fountain and listened to the customers as she poured cup after cup of coffee.

After I took a seat, a group of five women scurried in and claimed the last open booth. Before long the customers' connective conversations energized the room with discussions of work, kids, and local court cases, and their interactions evoked a sense of familiarity and shared understandings. The fountain clerk, Lou Thornton, continued to chat leisurely and to refill their cups.

Lou, after taking my order, quietly prepared first one request then the next. I overheard two of the men bidding their goodbyes because duty called them, and I watched them leave through the back door. When the small group of women sitting in the booth behind me followed suit, I took advantage of the situation and began a conversation with Mrs. Thornton.

Lou's manner became youthful as I asked her to reminisce about the drugstore. She first made mention of its history that dated back to the turn of the century when this building housed Flannigan's Dry Goods Store. Later in the 1930s, she recalled, a series of drugstores had offered their various businesses at this site. However, it was in 1953 that Jack Hall, a drug salesman from Oklahoma, bought the drugstore and brought in Gordon Rice as his partner and the business became known as H & R Drugs.

In 1964 Mr. Hall retired and Dean Paul Bennett joined Mr. Rice, but after Mr. Rice retired in 1977, Mr. Jerry Yocham, the current co-owner and pharmacist, joined Dean Paul to make it a venture run by two Hillsboro natives. In yet another changing of the guards, Dean Paul Bennett retired

and his son Stephen joined forces with Mr. Yocham.

Lou then reminisced about when, as a young woman, she had started working at the soda fountain in 1949. Softly she talked about her original plans to stay at that job for only a short while, but as fate would have it, she was named manager and has worked at the fountain ever since.

With that last bit of information, she pointed to the pharmacy where Jerry Yocham busily filled prescriptions, so I rose to speak with him. He confirmed Lou's information about the drugstore's history and after a slight pause added that he has watched over the years as the number of customers has diminished. He recalled how the store used to always be filled with people stopping by for sodas, sandwiches, and ice cream; however, when the Interstate bypassed the town, the number of people who patronized the town square business began to decrease.

On that last note I asked Jerry if he planned to keep the fountain open; he gave a nod and offered, "I'm going to try my best to keep it open. You know, it's a different world out there now and people need a comfortable, safe place where they can gather with their friends."

But as time passes on, apparently so do many of the comfortable, safe places where friends can gather. In the course of publication of *Counter Culture Texas*, H & R Drugs has closed its doors, and the once active fountain lies dormant.

STAR DRUG STORE

In July Galveston brims with tourists drawn to the island and town not only for its sandy beaches but also for its rich history. I guess you could say we were no different; we were typical tourists in search of a touch with the past. We strolled along the sidewalk on 23rd Street then made a broad sweep around a roofing crew that sweated under the blazing Texas sun. Once past the construction, we stepped up onto a raised sidewalk, and our eyes fell upon the Star Drug Store.

The second I opened the front door, a blast of arctic-cold air escaped, and simultaneously the man behind the large soda fountain greeted me. A glance about the place revealed that one-half of this enormous, box-like room was taken up by a soda fountain. It stood in the middle of the store, a Gulliver-sized, four-cornered island of festivity where fifteen people sat in little customer cliques and enjoyed food and drink. Thirteen unoccupied, single pedestal barstools waited for visitors to claim them.

The distinctive black-and-red stools appeared bold against the white tile that lined the counter's base. Clinking silverware serenaded soft voices as easy tones from a radio drifted over from one corner of the room. Overhead, six fans hung down from the thirty-foot ceiling and gently cooled the diners and wait staff.

I examined both the storefront windows and the large doors that stretched from floor to ceiling and invited the patrons' perusal of people passing by outside. My eyes then traveled to the mezzanine that encircled the room's upper balconies and was filled with antiques. Below that mezzanine stood glass cabinets built into the side walls, which were fronted by old display counters; they housed collections of Galveston memorabilia.

To learn about the historical building, a waiter directed me to Elliebeth Rogers. I watched as this energetic lady with the dark hair came to the end of the small tour she was giving to some interested tourists. Just as she closed a 1925 daily ledger filled with handwritten entries, she turned to the group and said, "If you find one of your relative's names in here, let me know and I'll gladly let you have that page for a keepsake." I made note of her generosity.

Soon Elliebeth and I sat together in one of the back booths and she began a brief history lesson on the Star Drug Store. Records show that in 1846 the original business was located at the corner of Post Office Street and Tremont, then it was moved in 1889 to this location. Skipping forward in time, she told me that the last major owner was a Mr. Clampett, and after his death around 1981 the building had stood vacant for almost eight years.

It was Elliebeth who breathed life back into the place when she bought the drugstore in 1989. "Think about it," she said, "I

Star Drug Store

bought a business that was already over one hundred years old. Can't get any better than that, can it?"

Although the building had fallen into great disrepair, she said that didn't stop her from buying it. Part of her decision was driven by some of her fondest memories, when as a little girl she and her friends had met at this very fountain to giggle, gab, and share a milkshake.

Elliebeth explained that once she bought the store, she knew it was the right thing to do. She perceived that the sense of community on the island waned somewhat during the 1970s and 1980s, and with the purchase of the business it was her opportunity to make the drugstore a place where she could "give back to the community instead of taking from it." Her final comment was that she believed it is a "respect for the art of antiquity" that brings people from all walks of life into the drugstore.

Unfortunately, the Star Drug Store is no longer open. A major fire in 1998 lowered this regal, historical building to its knees. Visitors today can only stand outside the store's charred structure and imagine the happy faces of those who once experienced the good fortune to sit around the grand counter and be a part of living history.

VICTORIA PHARMACY

Once we arrived in Victoria, we found several places to consider for the book, but the one that reeled us in and snared our full attention was Victoria Pharmacy located on East Rio Grande Street. A simple message posted under a handicap sign on the store caught my eye. It read, "honk for service," and we wondered if it meant what it said.

Stepping into the drugstore, I first noticed rows of wheelchairs and walkers, racks of gowns and robes, and bundles of canes and umbrellas. All of these items were mixed in with a wide selection of medical equipment. Somehow the sign out front seemed like it might be a fitting message for the store's customers.

I turned to the left and noticed a dining area that was closed. However, curiosity led me to check out the darkened alcove, and in that dimness I found it. At the front left of the dining room stood a single, horseshoe-shaped counter topped with bright red Formica and flanked by eight black vinyl barstools. Twelve booths paralleled the fountain's length and stretched to the far right of the dining area.

Mounted on the wall at the end of the room was a large blue marlin frozen in mid-struggle. Beneath this elegant sporting fish hung a framed picture of a tanned, young man who beamed victoriously beside his displayed catch. I was still staring at the picture and trying to imagine the man and the fish as they locked wills when I heard someone behind me.

I turned and watched as he strolled toward me. His long blonde-and-gray hair was pulled into a ponytail. His reading glasses dangled from a chain around his neck. His bright red suspenders contrasted a stark white shirt. And his gray pants were crammed into the tops of his black boots. Although this gentleman was many years older, B. E. Leissner exuded the same vibrant spirit captured in that youthful photo where he had stood beside his spoils.

He flashed a warm smile and asked if I needed anything, and after I explained my mission, he said he would be glad to help me out. With the flick of a light switch the room brightened and we sat down at one of the tables in the dining room. Energetically, Mr. Leissner talked about his father, Butler Leissner, who had opened this pharmacy in the 1940s as a service to the people. To further provide for his customers, B. E.'s father had also offered a beer garden with a weekly polka band for entertainment.

This piece of information seemed to tweak B. E.'s memory, and with a grin on his face he then shared that when he was nine years old he used to deliver prescriptions on a Shetland pony. He pointed out that although those Shetland pony deliveries no longer exist, the same caring philosophy does.

He returned to the history. In 1948 his father and Dr. Webb DeTar improved the pharmacy to offer more modern merchandise for an ever-aging population. In keeping with their desire to cater to their

customers, the two men took out the beer garden and replaced it with a car hop service. This explained the gargantuan carport that stood in front of the building.

B. E. explained that his role in the business definitely began after he was released from the army in 1955 and he returned to Victoria to help his father run the business. It was in 1971 that he increased his partnership in the venture when he helped his father expand the building.

With that B. E. pointed around the area in which we sat and recalled that he and his father had wanted this dining room to be a place where people could feel comfortable to congregate and share life stories. As if anticipating my next question, B. E. confirmed that the fountain is home to many loyal, longtime customers during certain hours of the day.

With that I asked about the "honk for service" sign, and B. E. grinned that ever youthful grin of his and offered this clarification. He spoke tenderly about the growing number of aging customers who couldn't get around as easily as they used to. So in an effort to help them out, the pharmacy urges the elderly to just "give a little honk" and B. E. or one of the employees will go to them. Then he talked about his fear that as the median age of his customers continues to rise, the pharmacy and its dining room will someday become a thing of the past.

I asked if he had any children who might continue the family business, and B. E. responded, "Well, I have seven children, but they're spread throughout the country and are all in successful businesses. So, I don't think any of them will come back home to run it."

Unfortunately, B. E. wasn't too far off the mark when he expressed his concerns about the pharmacy becoming a "thing of the past." About one year after this interview, Mr. Leissner closed the pharmacy's doors and auctioned off many pieces of his family legacy, consigning yet another page of Texas history to memory.

INDEX